CW00828254

ÖZLEM'S TURKISH TABLE

Recipes from My Homeland

with a tribute to
Southern Turkish Cuisine

ÖZLEM WARREN

Foreword by Ghillie Başan | Food Photography by Sian Irvine

My grandparent's 450-year-old family home in ancient Antioch, Antakya

ÖZLEM'S TURKISH TABLE

Recipes from My Homeland

with a tribute to
Southern Turkish Cuisine

ÖZLEM WARREN

Foreword by Ghillie Başan | Food Photography by Sian Irvine

Dedication

For my dear parents, Gülçin and Orhan, for their passion for Turkish cuisine and continuously inspiring us; and for planting the seeds of a love for good food and the joy of sharing to us. And also to my dear husband, Angus and our children Mark Can and Emma Gülçin, for all their love, support, patience and understanding.

Copyright

First published 2018
Published by GB Publishing.org
www.gbpublishing.co.uk
Copyright © 2018 Özlem Warren

ISBNs
978-1-912031-94-8 (hardback), 978-1-912031-93-1 (eBook)
978-1-912031-92-4 (Kindle)

Graphic Designer & Art Director: Holly Tillier

Food Photography: © Sian Irvine

Photographic Assistants: Jonny Baker & George House

Location Photographs:

© Claudia Turgut 2018 – *pages 13 - top and bottom, 15 - top left, 19, 20 - bottom, 22, 58, 66, 78,79, 92-93, 100, 108-109, 114-115, 142, 144-145, 155, 160-161,168, 169, 170, 196-197, 202-203, 207, 214-215, 229, 232-233, 240-241, 246-247, 253, 261 - top left, 268-269, 288-289, 302*

© Katherine Baker 2018 – *pages 8 - bottom right, 9, 20 - top, 206, 234, 304*

© Ismail Daşgeldi 2018 – *page 23*

© Nancy Laing 2018 – *pages 2-3, 14 - bottom right, 15 - bottom left, 24 - left, 261 - right column*

© Joy Ludwig-Mcnutt 2018 – *page 8 - top left*

© Julia Power, Turkey's for Life 2018 – *pages 26, 252*

© Lyn Ward, Fethiye Times 2018 – *page 236*

Photographs:

© Suphi Ural 2018 – *page 14 (black and white family photos)*

© Ozerlat UK 2018 – *pages 293, 296, 303*

© Nadia Swindell Photography 2018 – *page 10*

Food Stylist Assistants: Susie Bossard, Claire Fitzsimons, Ellie Harrison, Ann Holliday, Mina Hoad, Heleen Koolhof and Leonie Wright

Props Stylist: Sian Irvine

Copy Editor: Will Campbell

Associate Editor: Gillian Burns

With Thanks

Healthy generations have been growing up with Pınar for many years. Özlem's Turkish Table gives sincere thanks and gratitude to Pınar, for giving their support to this special book, sharing the riches of Turkish cuisine, and passing this on to future generations.

Since its establishment in 1973, Pınar has positioned itself as a leading brand in the food industry and offers products for those who are looking for the highest quality produce. In Turkey the Pınar brand is known for its innovations, particularly in the dairy, meat and soft drinks sectors.

www.pinar.co.uk
Facebook, Instagram, Twitter: @pinarfoodsuk

www.pinar.de
Instagram: @pinar_germany

www.pinar.com.tr
Facebook, Instagram: @pinarhepyanimda

No part of this publication may be reproduced, stored in a retrieval system or transmitted in any form or by any means without the prior written permission of the publisher.

Enquiries concerning reproduction outside of the scope of the above should be sent to the copyright holder. You must not circulate this book in any other binding or cover and you must impose the same conditions on any acquirer.

A catalogue record of the printed book is available from the British Library.

Ovens should be preheated to the specified temperatures.
We recommend using an oven thermometer. If using a fan-assisted oven, adjust temperatures according to the manufacturer's instructions.

Foreword

My love affair with Turkey and Turkish food has spanned more than 30 years and, over those years, it has found a culinary voice in numerous articles and a handful of books. There are few places in the world where the cuisine is so rich and diverse, where the people are so friendly and keen to share, and where the hospitality shines like a bright beacon. With her nostalgic stories of family feasts and growing up in the Antakya region - the land of pistachios, bulgur, red pepper sauce, hot red pepper, and pomegranate molasses - Özlem has managed to bring the culinary culture alive. Another title for her book could be "Swimming with Watermelons" as the image of her doing that as a child in the family courtyard fountain where she grew up is what stories are all about.

My own Turkish story began in the ancient city of Bursa where I worked for a year and then travelled the length and breadth of the country, often invited into the humblest of homes to sample the regional specialities of the Black Sea, where hazelnuts and anchovies rule the table; Eastern and Central Anatolia where special cheeses are stored underground, stews are cooked in earthenware urns and sealed with bread dough, and ancient noodle traditions pop up in different versions of mantı; and to southern Anatolia for a memorable week-long wedding ceremony with great family gatherings and a mesmerizing array of traditional dishes, such as the dried aubergine dolma filled with fine bulgur combined with chili and tomato paste and the infamous mother-in-law's köfte which involve sealing a spicy minced meat mixture inside the meat and bulgur shell to represent the sealing of the new-daughter-in-law's lips.

When I ended up working in Istanbul for several years, my office was perched high above Istiklal Caddesi on the top floor of an archaic building with an unstable, caged lift but the view was magnificent – right across the Bosphorus and the Golden Horn and out to the Marmara Sea with the sound of the Muezzin echoing across the water from all sides and the sight of great tankers from Russia ploughing through the city from the Black Sea. It was simply mesmerizing and reminded me every day how the great Ottomans must have felt at the height of their Empire with such strategic domination under their feet. From the Topkapı Palace, just across the water from my office, they ruled the seas and the trade routes for 500 years and their industrious cooks created a remarkable culinary legacy, the Saray (Palace) cuisine, which includes succulent dishes like sweet and savoury pastries, indulgent milk puddings, and stuffed vegetables cooked in olive oil.

Historically and culturally, Turkey is a fascinating country of extraordinarily beautiful landscapes, bountiful seas and rich agriculture which contribute to the fresh, healthy, vivid cuisine captured in this book with its refreshing emphasis on the cooking of the southern region, the Güney cuisine. With its geographical proximity to Syria and the Arab influence, the region is a melting pot of religious faiths, languages and culinary cultures culminating in a uniquely robust and spicy cuisine. 'Greet a Turk and you will eat' is a saying that is demonstrated by Özlem every day as she shares her passion for her Turkish cuisine in her classes and talks, in her blogs, and now in this precious book, *Özlem's Turkish Table* in which she proudly puts the cooking of her southern homeland firmly on the culinary map.

Ghillie Başan

Writer, broadcaster and food anthropologist, with highly-acclaimed books on the cuisines of Turkish, Middle East and South-east Asia

Contents

Teaching at the Istanbul Culinary Institute with my mother, Gülçin

My Turkish culinary journey

Merhaba, my name is Özlem; I was born and raised in Turkey and lived in this magical land for 30 years. I feel very fortunate to be a part of this rich and welcoming Turkish culture.

I grew up with an abundance of freshly prepared food and the importance of sharing was instilled in us since childhood. My mother, Gülçin, would cook a hot lunch and dinner from scratch every day; my dad, Orhan, would go to our local pazar, farmer's market at least a few times a week to get fresh, seasonal produce. We would all help mum to make the dishes and everyone, from extended family to friends would be warmly welcomed to our table at every opportunity, a tradition that was passed on to us from my grandparents in Antakya. Continuing this legacy, I am passionate about sharing the gastronomical and cultural riches of my homeland through its cuisine.

Moving abroad, after getting married, gave me this opportunity on a global scale. My culinary journey began in 2005 as a guest chef with the Central Market Cooking Schools in Texas – USA, teaching Turkish cooking classes in Austin, Houston and San Antonio. It was an amazing experience to share my home country's delicious and rich cuisine. My students' interest for my homeland also prompted me to branch out of my chef's kitchen and launch my Culinary and Cultural Tours to Turkey. Hosting private tours to Turkey allowed me to share the historical and cultural riches of my beautiful country from an insider's perspective.

Then my family's move to England in 2009 led to the launch of "Özlem's Turkish Table" (www.ozlemsturkishtable.com) - my Turkish recipe blog that enabled me to stay connected with both my homeland and Turkish food enthusiasts around the world. More than ten years on and my love for Turkish cuisine has opened up new and exciting opportunities such as providing a food and menu consultancy, my supper clubs/meze nights, teaching Turkish cookery workshops at JA University in Amman, Jordan; London's Divertimenti Cookery School, Blid & Hatton Gatherings Food Studio in Surrey, England, Central Market Cooking Schools in Texas, USA, Istanbul Culinary Institute in Istanbul, Turkey as well as bespoke teaching. I also had the pleasure to be a part of the Turkish Chefs of the World (Dünyanın Türk Şefleri) TV programme, aired on the Turkish national TV Channel, TRT, as well as in 37 other countries. Another career highlight has been participating at prestigious events such as the Taste of London (with thanks to the Turkish Tourism Board, UK) and various food festivals to promote Turkish cuisine and culture.

My Turkish heritage defines the person I am today. As a mother of two young children, it gives me great happiness to be able to share and pass down my family's traditions, especially the link between our love for Turkish food and having a sense of belonging to Turkish culture. These are the values I embrace and strive to make an integral part of my children's everyday lives.

Istanbul Zekeriyaköy Cookery Class

Introduction

Hoş geldiniz - My warm welcome to you from Özlem's Turkish Table

This book is my tribute to the diverse, scrumptious Turkish cuisine and it is a celebration of my southern Turkish roots with regional recipes especially from my home town of Antakya. My cooking has, and continues to be, inspired by this magical land and its people. Let me take you on a Turkish culinary journey – to learn, taste and enjoy for yourself the delicious foods of my homeland and along the way I hope you will feel the warmth and generous spirit of our Turkish culture.

This book is a compilation of my favourite classic Turkish recipes as well as regional specialities from southern Turkey, with their exhilarating aromas, smells and colours. They have been lovingly prepared and passed down to me from my mother and grandmother. I share the recipes in this book with you in the hope that you will cook, enjoy and in turn, invite others to your own table to share a Turkish meal together.

Love of food is a universal bond that ties our history, customs and rituals together; passing from one generation to the next to define our lives today. Turkish cuisine has evolved over thousands of years of traditions with influences from the Middle East, Balkans, northern Africa and beyond. Today in Turkey, food and meal times are still as much the focal point of daily life as in centuries past. With my roots going back to Antakya, southern Turkey, I grew up with the enriching influences and a glorious melting pot of cuisines. Central to Turkish cooking is delicious seasonal produce, wholegrains, legumes, meat, poultry and seafood, beautifully flavoured with the artful use of spices, herbs and natural condiments like pomegranate molasses, nar ekşisi and pepper paste, biber salçası. I count myself very lucky to have grown up with these enchanting tastes of southern Turkish cuisine and I'm excited to share this delicious slice of my homeland with you all in this book.

My dishes are naturally flavoured with olive oil, lemon juice, nuts, spices, and southern Turkish ingredients such as pomegranate molasses, nar ekşisi. I believe preparing dishes is a personal choice, so please use your own creative freedom to tweak a recipe to suit your own taste and use what's available in your pantry. I aim to show you how to prepare the healthy, delicious Turkish food through my easy-to-follow recipes in this book. I am glad to mention that Turkish cuisine also offers many options for those with vegetarian, gluten-free and vegan dietary requirements.

A typical Turkish meal starts with soup – a staple in everyday meals. There is always a plate of hot and cold mezes (small appetizers) on the table. Recipes may vary by region and dishes are based on what produce is fresh, in season, and available at the local market, pazar. For instance, a typical meal in our home may include the smoked aubergine/eggplant salad with tomatoes, onions, peppers – Patlıcanlı Ekşileme, a southern Turkish speciality, and tray bake spinach and cheese filo pastry – Ispanaklı Peynirli Börek; a huge favourite with children, as well as adults. This is often followed by a meat-based course, perhaps baked Turkish meatballs with vegetables – Fırında Sebzeli Köfte or a fish based course. And finally, there's always time for a sweet treat and we Turks love our dessert, whether it be freshly baked baklava, dried baked apricots with walnuts – Cevizli Kuru Kayısı Tatlısı, or a plate of fresh fruits. A Turkish meal always ends with Turkish coffee, Türk kahvesi or Turkish tea, çay; we take time to enjoy every single sip with family and friends around the table.

Hospitality plays a very important part of Turkish culture. There is an old Turkish saying "Başımın üstünde yerin var" which means "I place you at the top of my head." For me, this sums up Turkish hospitality perfectly. We Turks place guests first and foremost in our thoughts and always welcome guests with generous hospitality. I have fond memories of watching my grandmother placing an extra plate or two on the table in our family home in Antakya when I was a child, as someone would almost always stop by at mealtimes. They would be greeted with kindness, a plate of food, and the customary invite to join us - everyone was welcomed at our table. A special tradition we carry on with our family to this day. It is the Turkish way of showing that we care - to share meals with our family, friends and neighbours. And we feel no one should ever leave a Turkish table without feeling satisfied, full and happy.

Before I conclude, it's good to remember that Turkish cuisine reflects thousands of years of traditions. Therefore, sometimes it is hard to state the precise origins as to where a particular style of making a dish came from. For many recipes, many variations can be available. This can be seen in neighbouring cuisines from nearby countries such as Syria and Iran. Even within Turkey, the same dish may be interpreted in different ways, as well as at my home and at my mother's and grandmother's table in Antakya. Moreover, you may like to create your own version.

I hope my book introduces you to the many foods of Turkey and especially southern Turkish cuisine. May it inspire you to create, cook, and experiment, but most of all - enjoy the magnificent cuisine of my beautiful homeland, Turkey.

Afiyet Olsun,

Özlem

My parents Gülçin and Orhan's engagement at my grandparent's home in Antakya

Özlem with her mum, Gülçin and father, Orhan

My grandfather, Suphi Öğreten

My grandmother Nazime with her sister Nimet

My parents with my children, Mark Can and Emma Gülçin

My Turkish roots

My mother, Gülçin and my father, Orhan were both born in Antakya. My grandfather from my father's side, Ahmet, was a soap maker (my father's surname "Sabuncu" means "soap maker"); he was respected in Antakya for the quality of his olive oil soaps. My mother's father, Suphi, was a food merchant, trading fresh and dried produce within the city and across the border in Syria. I grew up with an abundance of fresh produce and remember the excitement of grandpa delivering cases of figs, aubergines/eggplants and tomatoes which we always shared with our friends and neighbours. That generosity and spirit of sharing was instilled in me by my parents and the community I was raised in – it is our Turkish way of life.

My grandparent's home in Antakya was a 450-year-old stone house where I spent many happy childhood holidays. The rooms were attached in an octagonal shape around a central courtyard and I remember being fascinated by the bird engravings on the stone walls and the doves who nested in the roof and sang. Pomegranate, fig and walnut trees provided the courtyard with a welcome shade from the summer heat and endless entertainment for a child eating a bounty of juicy figs and young walnuts with their soft white flesh. There was a small fountain in the courtyard where we put watermelons to chill. My cousins and I would swim and play in the cool fountain water alongside the watermelons – happy childhood days.

My grandmother would send us grandchildren on endless errands to buy cheese and yoghurt at the local dairy, or the city's historic vegetable and spice market, Uzun Çarşı, which fascinated me with its vibrant colours and flavourful aromas. But it was the trips to the bakery, fırın, that we loved the most. My grandma prepared fillings for Etli Pide or Biberli Ekmek, flat breads with various toppings at home and we would take it to the bakery to cook in his big ovens. Oh, how we looked forward to that first bite of hot fresh flat breads, with grandma's filling over them. I still remember that first bite of the pide all these years later!

My mother and grandma prepared lunch and dinner together every day whenever we visited. It was our family ritual at the end of the day to gather around the courtyard dinner table under the fig tree's shade where we would share an evening in conversation and laughter over plates of mezes, fruits, vegetables, savoury pastries and kebabs, delicious memories.

My parents Orhan and Gülçin, at our home in Surrey, England

Food made with love, an expression of love

Cooking is a way of life for me. Trying a new recipe, invariably starts with a phone call to my mother. This is to learn how she and my grandmother prepared the dish and to talk about the ingredients available in England, where I live at the moment. I often have to experiment and substitute different ingredients when the Turkish version isn't available. Mum and I will recall memories of cooking together, my dad's morning trips to the local market, pazar, for vegetables, and whoever was at home would help chop and prepare the next meal. I am grateful to have grown-up with this appreciation of food and the caring, nurturing, respectful spirit it inspired for one another.

For Turks, cooking and sharing a meal with family and friends is our way of showing our love and care – and as we say in Turkish, "Paylaştıkça artan mutluluk" - "Happiness that grows with sharing." My mother taught me to "Greet your guests always with a warm smile on your face and in your heart. Make them welcome and feel they are a part of our extended family." It is a lesson and value I live by every day.

Our family trips back to Turkey are always a cause for much excitement with my children – and needless to say, for me! On the plane journey, they always ask - "Will anneanne, grandma prepare the Big Dinner on the first night and will we all eat together?" Here "together" means the whole family - my sister's family, cousins, grandma and grandpa! My mother will have been cooking and preparing for days before our arrival making sure to include our favourite dishes. But it is the togetherness, the gathering of our family to share a meal that stays in my children's mind and heart the most. I will always remember my parents traveling to the USA when my children were born to help in their loving Turkish way – with food! My mother cooked every day for a month and when she left, there was another month's worth of meals in the freezer for us new parents. That was her way of expressing her love and it had been gratefully appreciated.

At home, it is customary to wish everyone we dine with "Afiyet Olsun," meaning "enjoy in good health." This is followed by a respectful tribute to the creator of the meal, as the guests say – "Elinize Sağlık," meaning "health to your hands for creating this meal."

My mother serving her festive meal with grandchildren Defne and Emma Gülçin

Turkish culinary history

Turkey is a geographical culinary treasure trove. The country is surrounded on three sides by the Aegean, Black and Mediterranean Seas. This fertile land stretches from east to west and is dotted with impressive mosques, ancient Roman ruins, colourful, vibrant markets, and a breathtaking landscape of mountains, lakes and a lace-like coastline. It is no surprise therefore that Turkey is described as the geographical and cultural bridge connecting Europe and Asia. On the eastern side - Turkey borders Syria, Iraq and Iran whilst its European neighbours lie to the west – all have had an indelible and profound impact on Turkey's history and its cuisine for thousands of years.

Turkish cuisine dates back to the 6th century AD.

Turks then were nomadic tribes in central Asia and their food was centered on meat, grains and dairy products – all are still an integral part of Turkish meals today. By the 11th century, Turkish nomads had settled in Anatolia, the land of the modern day Republic of Turkey. It was the formation of the Ottoman Empire in the 14th century, which provided a major contribution to Turkish cuisine.

Anatolia was host to many ancient civilizations from the Hittites, Lycians, Persians, Ancient Greeks, eastern Romans and then the formidable Ottoman Empire which spanned more than 600 years. Today's Turkish cuisine is a true "melting pot" and reflects the richness and diversity of all these ancient civilizations and their intertwined culinary traditions.

Turks in Ottoman times placed great importance on lavish dining and opulent entertaining. They conquered vast amounts of land and built huge palaces like the Topkapı Palace in Istanbul. The grand kitchens of the Topkapı Palace were housed in several buildings under ten domes. It is well worth visiting them when in Istanbul. By the 16th century, the Ottoman Empire was at its peak and the palace kitchens employed 1,300 staff serving more than 10,000 people per day. Chefs specialized in different categories of dishes, such as börekçi, savoury pastry chef; baklavacı, the maker of sweet pastries; turşucu, the pickle-maker and so on.

The palace kitchens had been a focal point at the Topkapı Palace; cooking was regarded as an art form and lavish banquets were prepared for the Sultan and his guests. It was also a means of conducting business and trade engagements in a civilized manner. During Ramadan and other religious festivals, food from the palace kitchens was also shared with the poor and the public. The Ottoman Empire stretched from the Balkans to southern Russia, across to the north African continent to the Middle East and was made up of many ethnic communities. Each contributed their own authentic ingredients and flavours to the palace kitchens which further enriched and expanded Turkish cuisine. The Sultan also controlled the spice route and demanded his merchants to trade only the highest quality ingredients. Walking through Istanbul's Spice Market, Mısır Çarşısı, today, you can still see the quest for the best quality in the rich variety of spices, dried fruits, nuts and more.

After the collapse of the Ottoman Empire, today's Republic of Turkey was founded by Mustafa Kemal Atatürk in 1923. Turkish cuisine today is an intriguing balance of the past and present – always honouring and preserving its heritage born from ancient Anatolian and Ottoman traditions whilst being open to the fast-moving changes of the 21st century.

Today's Turkish cuisine is based on fresh, seasonal produce and has a rich culinary heritage. Blessed with a fertile land, four distinct seasons and a diverse landscape, Turkish cuisine is rich on regional variations too. This book pays a special tribute to my hometown Antakya and southern Turkish cuisine, which we will look in more detail next.

St Peter's Church, Antakya

Hatay Archeological Museum

Antakya's History

My family's roots goes back to the ancient city of Antioch (today's Antakya at the southern end of Turkey), by the Syrian border. It is this special land that has inspired my cooking and I want to introduce this fascinating place to you briefly.

Antioch was founded by the Syrian King, Seleucus I Nicator, one of the Alexander the Great's generals in 4 BC. He named the city Antioch after his father, Antiochos. Antioch was one of the largest cities in the Roman Empire and the city was once called "the fair crown of the Orient." Antioch flourished due to its strategic location, its fertile land and being en-route to the Silk Road and eventually rivalled Alexandria as the chief city of the Near East.

Antioch was also a city of great religious importance, especially in Christian history; it was the base for Saint Paul's missionary journeys, where Jesus' followers were first called "Christians".

Dating back to 30 AD, Cave Church of St Peter in Antakya is thought to be the first Christian church outside the holy city of Jerusalem. Declared a place of pilgrimage by Pope Paul 6th, St Peter's Church attracts thousands of Christians worldwide every June.

Over the centuries, the city fell under Roman, Byzantine, Ottoman and finally French rule for a short period during the collapse of the Ottoman Empire. In 1939, thanks to Atatürk, Antakya became part of today's Republic of Turkey.

Being home to so many ancient civilizations, Antakya - like many parts of Turkey - resembles an open-air museum, with archaeological sites everywhere. Hatay Archaeological Museum in Antakya hosts an extensive collection of Roman and Byzantine era mosaics and is well worth visiting while in Antakya.

Antakya's Uzun Çarşı, Long Market

Antakya & southern Turkish cuisine | Essential Ingredients

Antakya has been a fusion of ancient civilisations and religions and this richness is reflected in its cuisine. Antakya and southern Turkish cuisine has been influenced over the centuries by the Romans, Ottomans and neighbouring Middle Eastern countries as well as the West – each have added their own richness and unique flavours. Influences from the Levantine cuisine, covering a large area of the Eastern Mediterranean, is especially evident in our shared love of meze. I am delighted that recently the Hatay province, with Antakya being the administrative capital, joined the select list of UNESCO Cities of World Gastronomy; a title that is much deserved.

Today, Antakya's cuisine is as diverse and cosmopolitan as the people that call this city their home. A mixed community of different ethnic backgrounds and religious faiths from the Vakıflı Armenian Village to Jews, Christians, Arab and Turkish Muslims - all living together peacefully for many centuries.

My uncle, like my grandfather, was a food merchant in Antakya, who celebrated Christmas and Hanukkah with his Christian and Jewish friends and during Ramadan he broke his fast with the Muslim community. I love hearing Antakya's streets filled with the church bells alongside the muezzin's call to prayer for Muslims at the mosque. I feel very fortunate to have grown up in a place that embraced and celebrated all these faiths living side-by-side.

And it is from all these people, their influences and their histories, that I draw inspiration for my cooking.

With this book, I hope to give a general introduction to southern Turkish cuisine, particularly Antakya cuisine; it's a rich cuisine with thousands of years of heritage and deserves volumes of books written to capture every element of it.

In Antakya and the southern region of Turkey, bulgur wheat, meat and yoghurt are everyday common staple ingredients. The spices take centre stage in Antakya cuisine and even a simple, everyday meal is flavoured with at least 2-3 spices. Dishes are flavoured with the artful use of spices such as zahter or za'atar, cumin, sumac, dried mint and pul biber, Turkish red pepper flakes.

Mezes – hot and cold dips, salads as well as savoury pastries are always one of the highlights of southern Turkish cuisine, with their inviting, refreshing aromas. For instance, flavoured with Antakya's delicious, aromatic olive oil, za'atar and pomegranate molasses, olive salad with pomegranate molasses and za'atar – Zeytin Üfeleme is a must in our home. Another speciality worth a mention is the walnuts and red pepper paste dip, Cevizli Biber or Muhammara, made with the region's pepper paste, biber salçası. This delicious dip always takes a place of honour at my mother's table whenever we get together with family and friends - a favourite with all generations.

Talking about southern Turkish cuisine, one needs to mention kebabs and regional specialities with meat and poultry, since they are as popular as the region's staple bulgur wheat. I grew up enjoying succulent homemade kebabs which were often cooked at our local bakery, fırın, in Long Market, Uzun Çarşı. Kebab mixture would traditionally be prepared at homes and then taken to the local bakeries to be baked in Antakya. I fondly remember taking my grandmother's tray bake kebab mixture, Tepsi Kebabı to our local bakery in Antakya to bake - delicious memories.

Southern Turkish cuisine, just like the rest of the country, has a rich variety of seasonal fresh produce to call upon when making a meal. As my grandfather was a food merchant, I grew up enjoying an abundance of ripe juicy tomatoes, figs, meaty peppers and many more. Patlıcan, or aubergine/eggplant deserves a special mention here. Aubergine/eggplant is ubiquitous and it's the most used produce in summer. In Antakya, locals would grill it, pickle it, smoke it, stuff it, use in the kebabs, salads and dips; they even make desserts using small, delicate aubergines. Drying aubergines, small red bell peppers and baby okra is common practice in southern Turkey – their rich flavours ensuring a constant year-round supply for casseroles and mezes in the cooler months. It is a wonderful sight to see long braids of colourful peppers and dark purple aubergines/eggplants hanging to dry outside village homes in the golden summer sun.

Last but not least, one needs to mention the region's sweet treats, especially my hometown Antakya's signature dessert of syrup soaked, cheese filled pastry strands, künefe. I remember as a child watching the delicate pastry strands being squeezed through a huge sieve at our local künefe shop in Long Market, Uzun Çarşı. My grandmother would prepare künefe in her garden as we waited excitedly for any leftovers of buttery soaked pastry strands. Antakya's kömbe cookies, shaped in intricately carved, wooden kömbe moulds as well as Gaziantep's world famous baklava, made with the region's glorious "green emerald" pistachios are among the sweet highlights of southern Turkish cuisine for me.

Ground Black Pepper

Turkish Red Pepper Flakes

Sumac

Nigella Seeds

Currants

Cumin

Dried Mint

Sesame Seeds

Za'tar Blend

Urfa Chillies

Wild Za'tar

Speciality Ingredients

Bulgur

Wholesome bulgur wheat is a major staple in any southern Turkish kitchen, often cooked daily; I love its nutty taste and texture. Bulgur wheat, unlike cracked wheat, is a grain made from cooked wheat berries which have the outer bran case removed, and are then dried and pounded. There are two varieties available, fine and coarse bulgur. Meals made with coarse bulgur are called "Aş" in Antakya and served as a main meal, such as in Kabaklı Aş, Bulgur pilaf with courgette/zucchini, onions and tomatoes – a huge favourite in our home.

Fine bulgur, ince bulgur is a finer ground and lighter in texture. We use fine bulgur in salads such as Spicy bulgur wheat salad with pomegranate molasses – Kısır, and specialities like oval bulgur balls with walnuts and minced/ground meat – Oruk.

Freekeh or firik

A super grain made from the unripened green durum wheat, freekeh or firik, as well call it, is popular in Antakya and in southern Turkish cuisine. The wheat kernels are roasted and rubbed to create its deliciously nutty, smoky flavour. Freekeh is packed with fibre and is usually paired with bulgur at my hometown. It is an ancient grain that has been part of Turkish and Middle Eastern cuisines for thousands of years. I love freekeh's earthy flavour and pair it with bulgur, meat and vegetables.

Red Pepper Paste - Biber Salçası

Antakya is renowned for its delicious red pepper paste, biber salçası - a rich paste made from juicy and spicy Turkish red peppers and it's an essential ingredient in southern Turkish cuisine. In my hometown of Antakya, village women cook huge batches of the freshly picked spicy red peppers and spread them out on top of their cloth covered terraces. Under the hot summer sun, the peppers dehydrate and their concentrated juices turn this paste into a robust flavour-packed condiment. Pepper paste is a versatile ingredient which is used to flavour casseroles, salads, dips, meat and vegetables. It is a must have item in my kitchen and a little bit of it adds so much flavour to any dish. It is available in Turkish and Middle Eastern stores and you can now be able to make your own red pepper paste at home with my recipe in this book.

Pomegranate Molasses - Nar Ekşisi

Another southern Turkish speciality is Pomegranate Molasses – Nar Ekşisi, made from the fresh pomegranate juice, which is reduced to a thick, rich molasses. I love its naturally sweet and tangy flavor. This concentrated flavour of pomegranates is a must for traditional salads like Kısır, Spicy bulgur wheat salad with pomegranate molasses and meze spreads. In Antakya, we also "bathe" our vegetables, such as aubergines, peppers and courgettes with a mixture of water and pomegranate molasses prior to stuffing them, as in the stuffed peppers and courgettes/zucchinis with bulgur and pomegranate molasses – Bulgurlu Dolma. The tangy, sweet molasses are absorbed into the vegetables for a unique, rich flavour. I included my recipe for homemade pomegranate molasses, nar ekşisi in this book, if you would like to make at home. Pomegranate molasses is also widely available in supermarkets and online these days.

A note on measurements

Quantities are provided in both metric and imperial measures. When measuring the ingredients, please follow one system throughout the book. All spoon measurements are level unless otherwise specified.

1 teaspoon	=	5ml
1 tablespoon	=	15ml
1oz	=	30g
1fl oz	=	30ml
1 (US) cup	=	240ml/8fl oz

British		US
Aubergine	=	Eggplant
Courgette	=	Zucchini
Minced meat	=	Ground meat
Coriander	=	Cilantro
Spring onions	=	Scallions

Commonly used spices and herbs

Tahini

Tahini or tahin as we call it, is an ingredient also widely used in southern Turkish cuisine. It's made from toasted, crushed sesame seeds and is used in a wide variety of recipes from dips such as hummus, salads, breads and cookies in Antakya. The creamy, rich and nutty flavour of tahini is a special favourite of mine.

Cumin

Ground cumin is widely used in southern Turkish cuisine. I love the pungent aroma of this ancient spice with its warm and slightly sweet flavour. Combined with chickpeas and tahini, cumin is the spice that makes hummus taste like, well, hummus. Cumin is wonderful on lamb, beef and chicken; as well as with chickpeas, lentils, cabbage, aubergine/eggplant and tomato.

Turkish red pepper flakes

Pul Biber, Turkish red pepper flakes is the most commonly used spice throughout Turkey. The juicy, spicy red peppers are dried then chopped, crushed and flaked into a coarse, almost ground mixture in southern Turkey. You will always see a small pot of red pepper flakes, pul biber, next to salt and black pepper on the tables of restaurants in Turkey. It has a delicious heat and a pleasant, smoky taste; it is available in various strengths and forms in Turkey. Although nothing tastes quite like the real thing, pul biber, Turkish red pepper flakes can be replaced with either chilli flakes or paprika.

Ground Black Pepper

Another ancient spice, used generously in Turkish cuisine is ground black pepper; it adds flavour, depth and warmth to every dish we cook. I freshly grind my black pepper for the best taste possible.

Zahter, or Za'atar

Zahter or also known as za'atar in the Middle East, is a popular herb as well as spice blend in southern Turkish cooking. The fresh version of zahter or za'atar looks more like summer savoury, or a cross between marjoram, oregano and thyme.

In my home town, Antakya, dried zahter blend is a rich mixture of crushed zahter herb, sesame seeds, crushed cooked chickpeas, cumin, nigella seeds, sea salt, sumac and many more. It is a real treat, and the locals not only use it for chicken and meat marination, in salads and pastries but they also enjoy their breakfast with this mixture. They simply dip their bread into olive oil, then into the zahter, a delicious treat.

Sumac

This is one of my favourite spices with its delightful fruity aroma and tangy flavour. Sumac is usually sold coarsely ground and slightly moist at home and adds a beautiful purple colour and a vibrant, lemony flavour to a dish. In fact, you can season food with sumac as you would with lemon or vinegar. Sumac is fabulous sprinkled on grilled fish, or on chicken before roasting, or in salads. I simply love it tossed with sliced raw onions, parsley and tomato, as in Piyaz Salad with tomato, parsley, onions and sumac – Soğan Piyazı .

Mint and dried mint

Mint is a versatile herb, commonly used in Turkish cooking; especially in salads, refreshing drinks like lemonade, stuffed vegetables and leaves. Dried mint is also popular particularly in southern Turkish cuisine and is liberally used in soups, salads, dips, bulgur based dishes as well as in casseroles. I adore the refreshing taste of dried mint – try cabbage with bulgur, minced/ground meat and spices - Bulgurlu Lahana Kapuska; dried mint flavours this dish so beautifully along with red pepper paste and Turkish red pepper flakes, pul biber.

Parsley

Flat leaf parsley (also called Italian parsley in the USA) is one of the most popular herbs used in Turkish cooking. It adds a clean and almost citrusy taste to food, yet it never dominates. It is the star of many salads, including Shepherd's salad, Çoban Salata and crowns soups, stews and mezes.

Dill

Fresh dill is a versatile aromatic herb commonly added to vegetables cooked in olive oil, Zeytinyağlı, stuffing for vegetables and as a flavourful garnish in mezes and dips.

Chapter One

Condiments

Home made condiments & Za'atar Blend

Home made red pepper paste
Biber Salçası

Makes
90ml/3fl oz/6 tablespoons

Ingredients

3 long red peppers
(or capsicum or bell peppers)

1 red chili pepper

240ml/8fl oz water

10ml/2 teaspoons sea salt

30ml/2 tablespoons olive oil

Biber Salçası, Turkish red pepper paste is a fundamental ingredient in southern Turkish cuisine. Even a teaspoonful of this delicious, deep red paste adds a rich flavour to dips, salads, marinades and casseroles. In my hometown of Antakya, village women cook huge batches of freshly picked spicy red peppers and spread them out on top of their cloth covered terraces. Under the hot summer sun, the peppers dehydrate and their concentrated juices turn this paste into a robust flavour-packed condiment.

Living abroad, I am unable to sun dry my peppers, so I make my own version of red pepper paste, biber salçası at home. It is a satisfying paste, simple to prepare and will greatly enhance any dish.

Method

Remove the seeds and stalks from the peppers and cut into quarters. Place peppers in a wide, heavy pan and add the water. Cover and cook over a medium heat, stirring occasionally for 35 minutes or until the peppers are cooked and the liquid has almost evaporated. Turn the heat off and allow the peppers to cool.

Once cool, peel off the outer skin and coarsely chop. Place in a food processor and process until the mixture is a coarse purée.

Note: I prefer mine on the chunky side – so no need to blitz.

Return the puréed peppers to the pan. Season with salt and cook over a medium heat for 10 minutes, stirring continuously so the pepper purée doesn't burn. Turn the heat to low; continue stirring and cooking for another 15-20 minutes, until the juices have evaporated. When the purée has a thick paste consistency, turn the heat off.

Pour the paste into a clean glass jar while still warm, top with olive oil and seal. When cool, keep your prepared paste in the fridge and use within two weeks.

Afiyet Olsun.

Home made pomegranate molasses
Nar Ekşisi

Makes 180ml/6fl oz pomegranate molasses

Ingredients

1lt/1.75 pints freshly squeezed pomegranates juice (out of 8 large pomegranates)

28g/1oz brown sugar

15ml/1 tablespoon lemon juice

The rich, tangy taste of pomegranate molasses, nar ekşisi is an essential ingredient in southern Turkish cuisine and is widely used in Middle Eastern cooking. This concentrated fruity syrup adds an exquisite flavour to salads, casseroles and dips.

Homemade pomegranate molasses, nar ekşisi, can be stored in an airtight container in the fridge for a month. The molasses will thicken as it cools and then sets in the fridge.

Method

Remove all the pomegranate seeds and save them in a bowl. Place a large bowl and a sieve in the sink.

Squeeze the pomegranate seeds with your hands through a sieve over the large bowl. Extract as much juice as possible. Discard the leftover seeds.

Pour the freshly squeezed juice into a heavy saucepan. Stir in the sugar.

Bring the pan to the boil over a medium to high heat and stir until the sugar is dissolved. Add the lemon juice, mix and reduce the heat to medium to low, just enough for simmering.

Simmer for about 70 minutes, stirring every 10 minutes; the juice will thicken and reduce in volume.

Turn the heat off and let the pomegranate molasses cool. It will thicken more as it cools.

Once cool, store in an airtight glass jar. The molasses will keep in the fridge for up to a month.

Afiyet Olsun.

Zahtar or Za'atar blend

Makes 6 tablespoons

Ingredients

30ml/2 tablespoons dried za'atar, dried wild oregano or marjoram (or regular oregano, if the wild version is not available)

15ml/1 tablespoon ground, cooked chickpeas

15ml/1 tablespoon sesame seeds

15ml/1 tablespoon ground sumac

10ml/2 teaspoons dried thyme

10ml/2 teaspoons ground cumin

10ml/2 teaspoons ground pistachio

10ml/2 teaspoons sea salt (please adjust to your taste)

5ml/1 teaspoon ground black pepper

Fresh Zahter or Zahtar is a popular herb grown in southern Turkey. It grows in abundance in the wild during the spring months in the regions around Kilis and Antakya. Fresh zahter has a small velvety leaf and looks similar to oregano, or a crossing of marjoram, oregano and thyme. This versatile herb is wonderful on salads like Zeytin Üfeleme, Olive salad with pomegranate molasses and zahtar (see page 103).

Za'atar is also the name of an exotic blend of herbs, spices and nuts, widely used in both southern Turkish and Middle Eastern cooking. In, Antakya, zahtar blend is generally made with dried zahtar leaves, sesame seeds, crushed cooked chickpeas, cumin, nigella seeds, sea salt, ground pistachio, sumac and more. I grew up with this rich, pungent spice blend and love its nutty-like texture. In Antakya, locals simply dip their bread with olive oil and then in this zahtar blend for a delicious breakfast.

This aromatic zahtar blend adds a lot of flavour when marinating meat, fish, poultry, cheese and vegetables. Zahtar can also be added in savoury pastries and flat breads. Here is how my family makes their zahtar blend at home.

Method

Combine all the ingredients in a bowl and mix them well. Rub well with your fingers (that will help to release their oil and aromas). Store za'atar or zahtar in a cool, dark place in a clean, glass jar, sealed tightly. When stored properly, za'atar can be used for a month.

Afiyet Olsun.

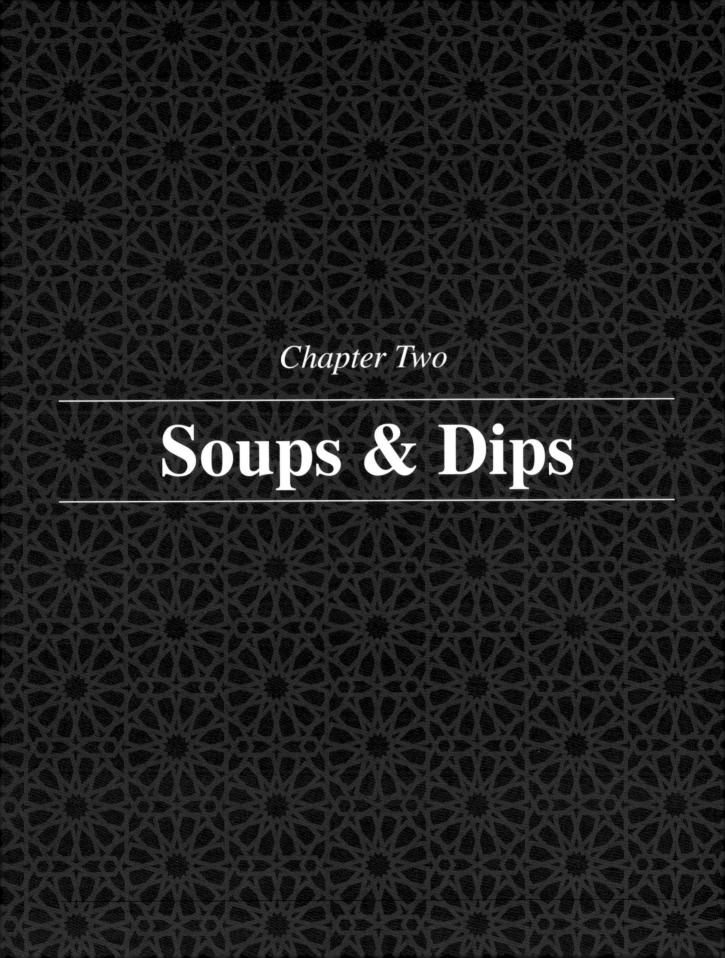

Chapter Two

Soups & Dips

Soups & Dips

Soups and dips have a special place in Turkish cuisine. Traditionally, meals start with a bowl of soup, çorba, followed by dips, hot and cold mezes. My dad always has soup with ekmek, Turkish bread, to start his meal, no matter how big or small the meal that lays ahead. Hearty soups such as Ezo Gelin Çorbası, spicy bulgur and lentil soup is also frequently served up as breakfast in the villages in Anatolia for a wholesome start to the day.

Turkish dips can be typically yoghurt, vegetables, nuts or pulses-based. Yoghurt has been a staple in Turkish cuisine, dating back to our origins in Central Asia; we love yoghurt so much that it is almost served with anything. Yoghurt's rich and creamy texture combined with fresh vegetables and herbs makes a delicious savoury side dish. The walnuts and red pepper paste dip, Cevizli Biber or Muhammara, from my hometown Antakya always hits the spot for me. This delicious dip always takes a place of honour at my mother's table whenever our ever growing extended family are around. It remains a favourite with all generations.

Spicy lentil and bulgur soup
Ezo Gelin Çorbası

Serves 4

Ingredients

290g/10oz split red lentils, rinsed and drained

1 onion, finely chopped

45ml/3 tablespoons coarse bulgur wheat, rinsed and drained

1.75 litres/3 pints water

60ml/4 tablespoons tomato paste

15ml/1 tablespoon Turkish red pepper paste

30ml/2 tablespoons olive oil

15ml/1 tablespoon dried mint

Juice of 1 lemon

Salt and freshly ground black pepper to taste

To serve:

15ml/1 tablespoon dried mint

5ml/1 teaspoon red pepper flakes/ paprika flakes

15ml/1 tablespoon olive oil

Lemon wedges to serve

This hugely popular spicy lentil and bulgur soup, Ezo Gelin Çorbası, is a hearty soup, rich in fibre and protein and highlights how we use spices to naturally flavour dishes such as the red pepper flakes and dried mint used in this recipe. The soup is named after the bride "Ezo", who impressed her in-laws when she made this heartwarming soup for them. This soup is so delicious and simple to make that you will want to make it again and again! It freezes very well, so I recommend making a big batch to enjoy for a warming lunch or supper at a later date. Red pepper paste, biber salçası, adds a wonderful, rich flavour to the soup.

Note: You can make your own red pepper paste, Biber salçası, with my recipe in this book if you like (See page 36, for the Red Pepper Paste recipe). If you prefer not to use red pepper paste, you can increase the amount of tomato paste to 5 tablespoons and the red pepper flakes to 3 teaspoons or even more, depending on how spicy you would like it to be.

Method

Heat the olive oil in a heavy, medium-sized pot and stir in the onions. Cook over a medium heat for about 2 minutes, stirring often, this will soften the onions. Add the lentils and the water. Cover and bring the pot to the boil. Cook over a medium to low heat for about 30-35 minutes, stirring occasionally.

Stir in the bulgur, tomato paste, red pepper paste and dried mint, season with salt and ground black pepper. Cover and cook for another 10 minutes, until the bulgur is cooked. Add some more water if the soup appears to be too thick. Pour in the lemon juice and mix well.

To serve, pour in 15ml/1 tablespoon olive oil in a small pan and stir in the dried mint and red pepper flakes. Stir and gently cook over a low heat for a minute. Pour in this sauce into the soup and combine well.

Serve the soup hot with lemon wedges aside.

Afiyet Olsun.

Red lentil soup with carrots and potatoes
Mercimek Çorbası

Serves 4

Ingredients

250g/9oz red lentils,
rinsed and drained

15ml/1 tablespoon long grain rice,
rinsed and drained

1 medium onion, finely chopped

1 medium carrot,
quartered and cut in small cubes

1 medium potato,
peeled and cut in small cubes

1.10 litres/2 pints hot water

30ml/2 tablespoons olive oil

15ml/1 tablespoon butter

10ml/2 teaspoons ground cumin

Juice of ½ lemon

Salt and ground black pepper
to taste

For the freshly made croutons:

3-4 slices of stale bread,
cut in small cubes

30ml/2 tablespoons olive oil

For the red pepper flakes
infused olive oil:

15ml/1 tablespoon Turkish pul biber,
red pepper flakes or paprika flakes

30ml/2 tablespoons olive oil

To serve:

Wedges of lemon

Mercimek Çorbası can probably claim to be Turkey's most favourite soup - as well as my father's! My mother and I both like to add carrots and potatoes to this nutritious soup. The bright colours of red lentils, carrots and potatoes bring a ray of sunshine to any cold winter's day. In southern Turkey, we use cumin and pul biber, Turkish red pepper flakes to add a warm, energizing flavour. I usually double this recipe and freeze the extra soup to be enjoyed when hungry on cold winter days.

Method

Pour in the olive oil into a large, heavy pan and stir in the onion, carrots and potato. Sauté for about 2 minutes, until onions start to soften. Add the lentils, rice and hot water to the pan. Bring to the boil and skim off any froth. Cover and simmer for about 30-35 minutes or until the lentils, rice and the vegetables are cooked. Stir occasionally to ensure the lentils don't stick to the bottom of the pan. Add a little more water to the pan if the soup appears to be too thick to your liking.

While the soup is cooking, place the cubed stale bread on a greased tray and drizzle the olive oil over them, make sure all the pieces are coated well. Grill for 2-3 minutes at a medium to high heat until they are golden brown.

Once the soup is cooked, add the lemon juice, butter and cumin to the mixture. Check the seasoning and add salt and ground black pepper to your taste, combine well.

In a separate pan, stir in the olive oil and the Turkish pul biber, red pepper flakes or paprika flakes and mix well over a low to medium heat. The red pepper flakes will infuse to the olive oil and this will taste spectacular in the soup.

Stir in the red pepper flakes infused olive oil to the soup, mix well. Serve the hot soup in individual bowls, with the freshly made croutons over the top and a wedge of lemon by the side.

Afiyet Olsun.

Yoghurt soup with rice, red pepper flakes and dried mint
Yayla Çorbası

Serves 4

Ingredients

150g/6oz whole grain basmati rice, rinsed

1.10 litres/2 pints hot water

15ml/1 tablespoon olive oil

500g/1¼lb plain, thick and creamy whole milk yoghurt

15ml/1 tablespoon plain, all-purpose flour

2 egg yolks

15ml/1 tablespoon dried mint

Salt and ground black pepper to taste

For the dried mint and red pepper flakes sauce:

30ml/2 tablespoons unsalted butter (you can use olive oil instead of butter, if you prefer)

5ml/1 teaspoon Turkish red pepper flakes or paprika – you can use more for a spicier flavour!

10ml/2 teaspoons dried mint

Yayla Çorbası is a yoghurt based soup that dates back to our Nomadic roots. Turks have been enjoying yoghurt since their early days of wandering. It is used widely in soups, dips, meat and vegetable marinades, and even in desserts like Revani. This humble, easy-to-make soup is beautifully flavoured with dried mint and red pepper flakes and, for us, it is a meal in itself. You can use long grain rice instead of basmati rice if you prefer.

Method

Bring the water to the boil in a heavy saucepan and add the rice and the olive oil. Stir well and simmer for about 20-25 minutes or until the rice is cooked. Turn the heat off.

Beat the egg yolks and combine with the yoghurt and flour in a large bowl. Beat until smooth (the flour and egg yolks stabilize the yoghurt and keep it from curdling). Take a couple of spoonfuls of hot water from the pan and blend into the mixture. Pour in the egg mixture to the soup, stir in the dried mint and season with salt and ground black pepper. Combine well and simmer gently for another 10 minutes, or until the soup has a creamy consistency.

To make the dried mint and red pepper flakes or paprika sauce, melt the butter in a separate pan over a low heat. Stir in the dried mint and red pepper flakes and blend gently on a low heat (so that the spices don't burn) for about 30 seconds. Pour this sauce into the soup, combine well.

Serve hot with a sprinkle of extra red pepper flakes if you like.

Afiyet Olsun.

Vegetable soup with orzo pasta
Şehriyeli Sebze Çorbası

Serves 4

Ingredients

1 onion, finely chopped

2 bell peppers (red, yellow or green), de-seeded and finely chopped

1 medium carrot, chopped into small pieces

180g/6¼oz orzo pasta

30ml/2 tablespoons of olive oil

400g /14oz/1 can of chopped tomatoes

10ml/2 teaspoons double concentrated tomato paste

1.10 litres/2 pints hot water

Handful of flat leaf (Italian) parsley, finely chopped

Juice of 1 lemon

Salt and ground black pepper to taste

10ml/2 teaspoons Turkish red pepper flakes or chili flakes to serve

Extra wedges of lemon to serve

Crusty bread or pide bread to serve

This vegetarian soup, Şehriyeli Sebze Çorbası, was a big hit with readers of my blog, Özlem's Turkish Table. Orzo pasta - or şehriye, as we call it in Turkish - thickens the broth to make the soup nourishing and comforting. As a fan of fresh lemons, I add a generous squeeze of lemon juice and plenty of red pepper flakes on top for a little extra heat and flavour.

Method

Heat the olive oil in a heavy, wide sauce pan and add the onions, peppers and carrots. Stir and cook for 2-3 minutes, they will start to soften up.

Pour in the hot water. Also stir in the chopped canned tomatoes and the tomato paste, combine well. Cover and bring to the boil. Stir the pot and cover again, cook for 15 minutes at a medium to low heat.

Then add the orzo pasta, season with salt and ground black pepper and combine well. Cover and cook for another 10 minutes on a medium to low heat, stirring occasionally.

Once the orzo pasta is cooked, stir in the parsley, pour in the lemon juice and mix well. Check the seasoning and add more salt and ground black pepper, if needed. Turn the heat off.

Serve hot with Turkish red pepper flakes or chili flakes over the soup, with extra wedges of lemon and fresh crusty bread or pide bread by the side.

Afiyet Olsun.

Walnuts and red pepper paste dip, Muhammara
Cevizli Biber

Serves 4-6

Ingredients

4 slices of white or whole meal stale bread (about 70g/2½oz)

⅓ small yellow onion, finely chopped

45ml/3 tablespoons Turkish red pepper paste, biber salçası

10ml/2 teaspoons concentrated tomato paste

225g/8oz walnuts, shelled

10ml/2 teaspoons ground cumin

Pinch of salt

60ml/4 tablespoons extra virgin olive oil

15ml/1 tablespoon water

To serve:

30ml/2 tablespoons extra virgin olive oil

5ml/1 teaspoon red pepper flakes to decorate

5ml/1 teaspoon ground cumin to decorate

Pita bread, pide bread or crackers to serve

This is a much loved dip and popular with everyone I have prepared it for. It is easy to make and has an earthy, moreish flavour that makes you want to come back for even more. Cevizli Biber, also known as Muhammara, is one of my mother's signature recipes and this version comes from her historic hometown Antakya, (ancient Antioch), and is part of every family get together. Whenever I make it abroad, I feel I am back home. There are variations of this delicious dip all around the Middle East.

Stored in an airtight container, this dip can be kept in the fridge for 3-4 days. Turkish and Middle Eastern stores carry the Turkish red pepper paste, biber salçası or you can make your own with my recipe in this book (see page 36).

Method

Ground the walnuts with the onion, cumin, salt, red pepper paste and tomato paste in your food processor. Soak the bread into water and squeeze out the excess water. Crumble the bread and add to the mixture in the food processor. Pour in the extra virgin olive oil and water and blend to make a smooth spread. If it appears to be too thick, add a little more olive oil.

Place the spread on a small serving plate or bowl. Drizzle the extra virgin olive oil all over and decorate with red pepper flakes and ground cumin. Serve the spread with pita bread, Turkish pide bread or crackers.

Afiyet Olsun.

Warm hummus with red pepper flakes infused olive oil
Humus

Serves 4

Ingredients

225g/8oz dried chickpeas, soaked in water overnight OR equivalent amount of pre-cooked chickpeas in can, drained and rinsed

5ml/1 teaspoon salt

60ml/4 tablespoons extra virgin olive oil

30ml/2 tablespoons water

1 garlic clove, crushed - optional

Juice of 1 lemon

30ml/2 tablespoons tahini

10ml/2 teaspoons ground cumin

To serve:

30ml/2 tablespoons olive oil

5ml/1 teaspoon Turkish red pepper flakes, chili flakes or paprika

½ teaspoon ground cumin to decorate

Slices of pita bread or Turkish pide bread to serve

This ever so tasty hummus is delicious, healthy and is always a part of our family's daily lunch spread. In southern Turkey, hummus is served warm with red pepper flakes infused olive oil or sautéed pastırma slices (Turkish dried cured beef coated with spices). I would urge you to try warm hummus this way, as the pungent cumin transforms the taste to a whole new level.

Please adjust the hummus recipe according to your taste - some prefer more garlic, while others like more tahini or lemon in it. This warm hummus makes a terrific appetizer to share; it also complements any grilled meat or vegetable well.

Method

If using dried chickpeas, soak the dried chickpeas in cold water overnight. Then drain the chickpeas and transfer them to a pan with plenty of cold water. Bring to the boil and cook for a few minutes. Then lower the heat and partially cover the pan. Simmer the chickpeas for 1 hour, until they are soft and easy to mash.

If pre-cooked chickpeas are used, drain the juice and rinse. Put the pre-cooked (or cooked) chickpeas in a food processor and blitz them together with the extra virgin olive oil, water, lemon juice, garlic (if used) and tahini. If it appears thick and difficult to blend, add a little more olive oil. Season with salt and stir in the cumin. Process until you achieve a soft, smooth paste. Cover and refrigerate until required.

Just before serving, warm the hummus in a small non-stick pan for a couple of minutes. In a separate pan, heat the olive oil gently and stir in the red pepper flakes. Combine for a minute or two and let the red pepper flakes infuse to the olive oil. Place the warm hummus in a plate or a bowl and drizzle the red pepper flakes infused olive oil all over. Sprinkle some extra ground cumin over the top. Serve with pita bread or Turkish pide bread.

Afiyet Olsun.

Spread of tomatoes, onions, peppers with red pepper paste
Ezme

Serves 4

Ingredients

4 medium-sized ripe tomatoes, halved and seeds removed

1 medium onion, finely chopped

2-3 small spicy pointy green peppers (use less or more depending on how spicy you like)

15ml/1 tablespoon red pepper paste

15ml/1 tablespoon tomato paste

Juice of ½ a lemon

Handful of flat leaf parsley, finely chopped

Handful of fresh mint leaves finely chopped

30ml/2 tablespoons extra virgin olive oil

Salt and freshly ground black pepper to taste

30ml/2 tablespoons crushed walnuts to serve (optional)

Hailing from southern Turkey, Ezme is a familiar spread that is served in kebab houses throughout Turkey and further afield. With a touch of red pepper paste, biber salçası and extra virgin olive oil, these simple yet fresh ingredients produce a surprisingly complex flavoured dish. Ezme can be made ahead of time and stored in the fridge to use later when entertaining.

Though not traditional, I like to sprinkle a few walnuts on my plate of Ezme for their sweet, nutty texture. It is now easier to source Turkish red pepper paste, biber salçası or better still you can make your own with my recipe in this book (see page 36, for the Red Pepper Paste recipe).

Note: In place of red pepper paste, you can increase the tomato paste to 30ml/2 tablespoons and add 10ml/2 teaspoons red pepper flakes or chili flakes for a delicious heat.

Method

Combine the red pepper paste and tomato paste with the onions in a bowl. Knead and mix them well with your hands so that the paste infuses to the onions (this also softens the onions and makes them even more palatable).

Stir in the tomatoes, peppers, parsley and mint, combine well. Drizzle the extra virgin olive oil and lemon juice over. Season with salt and ground black pepper and give them all a good mix. Cover and keep in the fridge until serving. It would be best if you can let the Ezme sit for an hour or so before serving; this will help the flavours mingle and settle.

To give this spread a more modern twist, I like to sprinkle a few crushed walnuts over Ezme when serving.

Afiyet Olsun.

SELÇUK BELEDİYESİ
FİYAT ETİKETİ

1 KiLO
1. TL

Diced cucumbers, yoghurt and dried mint dip
Cacık

Serves 3-4

Ingredients

*225g/8oz natural,
creamy plain yoghurt*

*1 garlic clove, crushed with salt
and finely chopped (optional)*

*About 100g/3½oz cucumber,
finely chopped*

5ml/1 teaspoon dried mint

Salt to taste

Fresh mint leaves to garnish

Yoghurt is a key ingredient in Turkish cuisine and some of the finest yoghurt in the world is made in Turkey. It is included with one dish or another at most meal times. My children always have a spoonful of yoghurt with their meals.

I love this Cacık dip; the cool cucumbers, yoghurt and dried mint combination makes a delicious, refreshing dip, served by the side of grilled meats, vegetables and casseroles. Traditional Cacık is a sort of chilled yoghurt soup with water and ice cubes added. Served in a small bowl with hot meal dishes, it refreshes and cleanses the palate. I prefer to serve Cacık as a mildly flavoured cooling dip without the water as in this recipe.

Method

Combine the yoghurt and garlic (if using) and beat until smooth. Stir in the chopped cucumber and dried mint. Add salt to taste, cover and refrigerate until required. Add fresh mint leaves for garnish when serving.

Afiyet Olsun.

Chapter Three

Hot & Cold Mezes

Hot & Cold Mezes

Mezzes, or meze, as they are known in Turkey, are small flavourful bitesize dishes that play an important role in everyday meals throughout Turkey. Originating from the Persian word mazzeh or mazze which means "pleasant taste, snack," mezes were designed to "wet" the appetite before moving on to the main course. Mezes can be dips, salads, savoury pastries or vegetables cooked in olive oil – all displayed in small plates to be shared. They can be enjoyed alongside ayran, Turkish yoghurt based drink, or rakı, an anise flavoured spirit, or beer or wine. I love the sharing element of the meze feast; gathering with friends and family and enjoying these delicious small platefuls together is my favourite part of any get-together. Based on seasonally available produce and changing from region to region, the varieties of meze dishes are endless and can be a meal in itself. Packed with flavour, wholesome and easy to make, mezes also offer delicious choices for vegetarian, vegan and gluten-free diets.

Sautéed carrots and parsley with garlic yoghurt
Sarımsak Yoğurtlu Havuç

Serves 4

Ingredients

3 medium carrots, coarsely grated

2 cloves of garlic, crushed in sea salt and finely chopped

450g/1lb natural plain yoghurt (whole milk yoghurt recommended)

30ml/2 tablespoons olive oil

Handful of flat leaf (Italian) parsley, finely chopped

Salt and freshly ground black pepper to taste

Sweet, mildly flavoured carrots mixed with garlic yoghurt can be served in several different ways – as a meze with pide bread or as a side dish with grilled meat and vegetables. In addition to meze spread, I like to serve this dish with lamb kebabs with pistachios and roasted vegetables, Fıstıklı Kebap (see page 199 for the recipe).

You can prepare this meze ahead of time and store the leftovers in the fridge for up to 2 days.

Method

Heat the olive oil in a wide heavy pan and sauté the grated carrots for 3-4 minutes, until they are about to soften up, but still a little crunchy. Turn the heat off and leave them aside to cool. In the meantime, stir in the chopped garlic into a large bowl of yoghurt. When cooled, combine the sautéed carrots into the yoghurt bowl and give a good mix. Stir in the chopped parsley and season with salt and ground black pepper, combine well.

You can serve this wonderful meze with slices of pide, flat bread, pita bread or crackers, or with sliced vegetables like celery, broccoli, and cauliflower to dip in. It also complements grilled meat, kebabs and vegetables beautifully.

Afiyet Olsun.

ADANA

KÖY

PATLICAN

Baba ghanoush; burnt aubergines/eggplants, peppers & tomatoes with pomegranate molasses | *Abagannuş*

Serves 4

Ingredients

2 medium aubergines/eggplants

1 pointy red pepper or bell pepper

3 small, ripe tomatoes

1 clove of garlic, crushed with salt and finely chopped

Juice of ½ lemon

30ml/2 tablespoons extra virgin olive oil

10ml/2 teaspoons pomegranate molasses, nar ekşisi

Salt and freshly ground black pepper to taste

This delicious meze, Abagannuş or Baba ghanoush, is popular in Antakya and southern Turkish cuisine and this version with tomatoes and peppers is our very own family favourite. There are many variations of Baba ghanoush throughout the Middle East - sometimes, tahini is used or plain yoghurt. What ingredients to use, or not to use, may invite heated debates! Aubergines/eggplants are traditionally cooked over an open fire or a burner to give them their smoky flavour. The skin of aubergines/eggplants and peppers burn and the flesh inside becomes soft, sweet and tender.

I like adding a light dressing of pomegranate molasses to balance with the aubergine's/eggplant's smoky flavour and enjoy it with crackers and feta or a sharp cheese on the side. When in season, sprinkle pomegranate seeds on top of the salad for a refreshing crunch. Serve Abagannuş with your meze spread or grilled main course.

Method

Place the aubergines/eggplants and pepper directly over the burner on a medium heat and roast for about 30 minutes (depending on the size of the aubergines/eggplants), turning occasionally (you can roast the tomatoes on a barbeque or in the oven at 200°C/400°F/Gas Mark 6 for about 20-25 minutes, as it can get quite messy over the burner).

While cooking over the burner, use metal tongs to turn the aubergines/eggplants and pepper around so that all sides cook evenly and the skin is nicely chargrilled. Cook until the skin is burnt and the flesh is soft.

Remove the cooked aubergines/eggplants, tomatoes and the pepper to a colander to allow them to cool. Once cool, peel and discard their burnt skin, remove the seeds of the pepper and cut the stalks of the aubergine/eggplant and pepper. Leave them in the colander to drain the aubergine's/eggplant's bitter juices. I like to gently squeeze the aubergine/eggplant flesh to drain as much fluid as possible.

Chop the flesh of the aubergine/eggplant, pepper and tomatoes coarsely and mash them with a fork. Place the flesh in a bowl and stir in the chopped garlic, lemon juice and the extra virgin olive oil, combine well. Season with salt and freshly ground black pepper.

When serving, drizzle over with pomegranate molasses and give a gentle mix; its tangy flavour works really well with the smoked aubergine/eggplant, peppers and tomatoes.

Afiyet Olsun.

Calf's liver with red onion, parsley & sumac piyaz salad
Arnavut Ciğeri

Serves 4

Ingredients

500g/1¼ lb fresh lamb's or calf's liver

60ml/4 tablespoons light olive oil

45ml/3 tablespoons all-purpose (plain) flour

10ml/2 teaspoons red pepper flakes or chili flakes

Salt and freshly ground black pepper to taste

For the red onion, parsley and sumac piyaz salad:

1 large red onion, cut in half lengthways and thinly sliced

Handful of flat leaf (Italian) parsley, coarsely chopped

10ml/2 teaspoons ground sumac

1 lemon cut in wedges to serve

This sautéed calf's liver is a popular Turkish meze and can also be served as a main course. Also known as Ciğer Tava in Turkey, it is an easy and delicious way to enjoy liver. Liver is not to the taste of everybody. But, let me try to change your mind with this recipe.

The calf's liver is a super-food; it is a good source of Vitamin A and six of the B Vitamins and folate. I like to squeeze fresh lemon juice on top just before serving – and am always happy when even those who normally pass on liver, enjoy this way of preparing. I used calf's liver but you can also use lamb's liver if available.

Tip: The trick with cooking liver is that it needs to be stir fried quickly for a few minutes each side so it browns slightly and gets crispy outside but stays moist and soft inside. So please prepare your red onion, parsley and sumac piyaz salad first and then cook the liver so that you can serve straight after cooking over the salad, with a wedge of lemon at the side.

Method

Make the piyaz salad first. Slice the red onion and rub 5ml/1 teaspoon salt (preferably sea salt) into the onion slices; this will soften the onions and make them more palatable. Stir in the chopped parsley, ground sumac and ground black pepper, combine well. Spread the piyaz salad on a serving dish and set aside.

Slice the liver into chunky bites or stripes (removing the skin or ducts). Spread the flour on a tray and stir in the red pepper flakes, salt and ground black pepper, mix well. Toss the sliced liver into the flour mixture and make sure all the liver pieces have a light coating of the flour mixture.

Heat the light olive oil in a wide, heavy pan. In the meantime, place absorbent kitchen paper towel on a clean tray. Toss in the liver into the hot pan with olive oil and sauté on a high heat for about 2-3 minutes each side. The liver pieces will become crispy and have a light brown coating outside but will still be moist and soft inside. Once cooked, remove with a slotted spoon and drain on the kitchen paper towel.

Serve immediately over the bed of red onion, parsley and sumac salad. We like to serve it with a wedge of lemon at the side and squeeze the lemon juice over the delicacy while eating; it gives a lovely refreshing taste to the liver and complements the red onion salad well.

Afiyet Olsun.

Circassian chicken with walnut sauce
Çerkez Tavuğu

Serves 6

Ingredients

225g/8oz chicken breast and 225g/8oz chicken thighs, trimmed of excess fat and cut into chunks

1 medium onion, coarsely chopped

200g/7oz walnuts, crushed

4 slices of stale bread, crusts removed

3 cloves of garlic, crushed with salt and finely chopped

10ml/2 teaspoons Turkish red pepper flakes, paprika or chili flakes

1 small bunch of coriander/cilantro or parsley, chopped

Salt and ground black pepper to taste

To serve:

30ml/2 tablespoons olive oil

5ml/1 teaspoon Turkish red pepper flakes, paprika or chili flakes

60g/2oz coarsely chopped walnuts

Handful of roughly chopped coriander/cilantro or parsley

Çerkez Tavuğu comes from the Ottoman Palace kitchens. Circassian women who served in the Ottoman harems, brought this dish with them to the Topkapı Palace, the residence of the Ottoman Sultans. Çerkez Tavuğu was originally made with fresh coriander/cilantro leaves, which is used widely in Circassian cuisine. I love the flavour of coriander/cilantro with this walnut sauce, but parsley is traditionally used as an alternative in Turkey. Either works well with this dish.

This is a tasty dish for lunch or a light supper, served with Shepherd's Salad, Çoban Salatası. You can also be frugal and make the best use of your leftover chicken roast with this walnut sauce to make and spice-up another satisfying meal.

Method

Combine the chicken thigh and breast, the onion and water to cover the chicken in a large, heavy pan. Season with salt and ground black pepper, cover and cook over a medium heat for about 35 minutes or until the chicken is cooked. Then turn the heat off. Remove the chicken from the pan and set aside to cool, keep the cooking liquid. When the chicken is cooled down, remove any skin, tear chicken pieces into thin strips and place in a large plate.

For the walnut sauce, soak the bread in a couple of tablespoonfuls of the cooking liquid. Squeeze and crumble the bread into a large bowl with walnuts, garlic, salt and red pepper flakes. In a food processor, combine these together to form a paste. Add more cooking liquid, a spoonful at a time until you reach a creamy consistency. I like to have small chunky bites of walnuts in the paste, rather than completely smooth. Stir in the chopped coriander/cilantro or parsley. Check the seasoning and add salt and ground black pepper if needed and mix well. Combine the chicken strips with the walnut dressing. Place on to a serving plate.

Just before serving; heat the olive oil in a small sauce pan and add the Turkish red pepper flakes, paprika or chili flakes. Stir and cook gently for about 30 seconds. Sprinkle chopped walnuts over the chicken, along with chopped coriander/cilantro or parsley. Then drizzle the warm, red pepper flakes infused oil over it and serve.

Afiyet Olsun.

Baked mini Turkish meatballs in tomato & red pepper sauce
Mini Sebzeli Köfte

Serves 6

Ingredients

225g/8oz minced (ground) beef

225g/8oz minced (ground) lamb

1 medium onion, grated

2 eggs

1 bunch of flat leaf (Italian) parsley, finely chopped

1 red bell pepper, diced

3 garlic cloves, finely chopped

400g/14oz (1 can of) chopped tomatoes

30ml/2 tablespoons olive oil

240ml/8fl oz water

Salt and freshly ground black pepper to taste

Small bowl of water with a drizzle of olive oil to shape the köftes

These homemade mini meatballs, köftes, was one of my favourite meals during my childhood. I am pleased to say that they are still a family favourite with my own children. They are easy to prepare and the pleasant aromas of köfte baking fills the kitchen. These baked mini köftes are enjoyed as a hot meze at home and at kebab eateries.

Serve with a meze spread or larger portions make a superb evening dinner with rice and steamed vegetables.

Method

Preheat oven to 180°C/350°F/Gas Mark 4

In a large bowl, combine the grated onions, eggs and parsley and knead well. That will help soften the onions and blend the ingredients.

Stir in the minced (ground) meat, season with salt (about 1-2 teaspoons) and ground black pepper to your taste. Knead for a good 3-5 minutes with your hands, until the mixture becomes elastic and has mixed well. Cover this meat mixture with cling film/plastic wrap and let it rest in the fridge for at least 30 minutes.

In the meantime, heat the olive oil in a heavy pan and stir in the garlic and diced bell peppers. Sauté for 4-5 minutes, while stirring often. Pour in the chopped tomatoes and water. Season with salt and freshly ground black pepper. Stir, cover and simmer on a medium to low heat for 10 minutes. Then turn the heat off.

Take out the meat mixture from the fridge to shape the meatballs. Have a small bowl of water with a drizzle of olive oil near you. Wet your hands with the water and take a small walnut size of the meat mixture and roll into a ball. Place the meatballs on a baking tray ready to cook side-by-side and continue until all the meat mixture is shaped into mini köftes, meatballs.

Bake the mini köftes in the pre-heated oven at 180°C/350°F/Gas Mark 4 for 25 minutes, they will start to get a nice golden brown coating.

Transfer the baked mini köftes in a large baking dish and pour in the pepper and tomato sauce around them, give them a gentle mix. Bake the mini köftes in tomato and pepper sauce for a further 15 minutes. The sauce will thicken, the flavours will blend in and the meatballs will have a wonderful coating.

Serve hot as part of your meze spread or with plain rice and Cacık dip of cucumber, yoghurt and mint if you like.

Afiyet Olsun.

Chapter Four

Salads

Salads

Turkish gastronomy is based on fresh, seasonal produce. I can happily spend a whole day wandering around the stalls of our local pazar, farmers market, in Istanbul with every stall arranged to showcase that day's freshly picked produce. Blessed with a seasonal variety of fruit and vegetables, we have a wide range of salads in Turkish cuisine. Our salads offer tempting, wholesome choices for vegetarian, vegan and gluten-free diets too. I hope you enjoy some of my favourite salads along with regional specialities from southeast Turkey.

Spicy bulgur wheat salad with pomegranate molasses
Kısır

Serves 4

Ingredients

350g/12oz fine bulgur wheat

1 medium onion, finely chopped

240ml/8fl oz hot water

15ml/1 tablespoon tomato paste

15ml/1 tablespoon red pepper paste, biber salçası

5ml/1 teaspoon red pepper flakes, chili or paprika flakes

Juice of 1 lemon

30ml/2 tablespoons pomegranate molasses, nar ekşisi

45ml/3 tablespoons extra virgin olive oil

4 spring onions/scallions, finely chopped

3 medium, ripe tomatoes finely chopped

A small bunch of flat leaf (Italian) parsley, finely chopped

5ml/1 teaspoon salt

Freshly ground black pepper to taste

Lettuce leaves to serve

Pomegranate seeds to serve

Kısır is a delicious salad made with fine bulgur wheat and packed with goodness – a real bowl of health. It is a hugely popular speciality and a "welcome salad" in southern Turkey though you might see variations throughout Turkey. Antakya's Kısır is prepared with the region's local pomegranate molasses, nar ekşisi and red pepper paste, biber salçası - both add a tasty depth of flavour to this salad. Pomegranate molasses is not so difficult to get a hold of now in supermarkets. But to impress – try to make your own with my pomegranate molasses recipe (see page 37). Turkish red pepper paste, biber salçası can also be made from scratch with my recipe (see page 36).

Kısır can be made a day ahead and stored in the fridge for a good few days. I personally think it tastes better the next day, as the flavours blend together. I like to serve Kısır with pomegranate seeds when in season and over lettuce leaves, as part of my meze spread.

Method

First mix the fine bulgur wheat, salt, ground black pepper, red pepper flakes, tomato paste, red pepper paste and the chopped onion and knead thoroughly – this will help all the flavours marry and the onion to soften. Pour the hot water over this mixture and stir, then leave to stand for about 15 minutes. The bulgur mixture should absorb all the water by the end of this period and will be of a dry consistency.

Add the lemon juice and the pomegranate molasses together with the extra virgin olive oil and knead well again. Stir in the spring onions/scallions, tomatoes and parsley and combine well.

Serve Kısır in a bowl garnished with pomegranate seeds and lettuce leaves. You can also place a spoonful of Kısır on each lettuce leave and serve to your guests this way.

Note: There are two main varieties of bulgur wheat available, fine and coarse bulgur. Fine bulgur is commonly used in salads whereas the coarse bulgur is used in pilafs or Aş as we call it in Antakya. If you can't get the fine bulgur wheat, you can make this salad with coarse bulgur. In that case, use 240ml/8fl oz hot water for 175g/6oz coarse bulgur and cook on a low heat for 10 minutes, covered.

Afiyet Olsun.

Piyaz Salad with tomato, parsley, onions & sumac
Soğan Piyazı

Serves 4

Ingredients

3 medium tomatoes quartered and coarsely chopped

1 red onion, halved and thinly sliced

1 bunch of flat leaf (Italian) parsley, roughly chopped

Juice of 1 lemon

Pinch of salt

30ml/2 tablespoons extra virgin olive oil

10ml/2 teaspoons ground sumac

5ml/1 teaspoon red pepper flakes, chili or paprika flakes (optional)

Freshly ground black pepper to taste

This vibrant and healthy Soğan Piyazı salad is quick and easy to prepare. It is traditionally served with kebabs or lahmacun, Turkish thin pizza with a minced meat topping. I like to flavour this salad with the tangy sumac; a popular southern Turkish and Middle Eastern spice that is sprinkled over meat, fish and salads. Its tart, citrusy flavour works well with the red onions and tomatoes in this salad. You can also serve this salad with cheese, olives and hummus with flat breads, pide bread or pita bread on the side.

Method

Rub sumac and the salt into the onion slices with your hands really well (this will soften the onions and help the sumac to infuse well). Stir in the chopped tomatoes, parsley and red pepper flakes, chili or paprika flakes (if used), combine well.

Whisk together the extra virgin olive oil and lemon juice and pour over the Soğan Piyazı salad. Season with more salt (if needed) and freshly ground black pepper.

Serve Soğan Piyazı salad with feta cheese, olives and/or hummus for a delicious spread. This salad is also the ultimate accompaniment of grills and kebabs.

Afiyet Olsun.

Smoked aubergine/eggplant salad with tomatoes, onions, peppers
Patlıcanlı Ekşileme

Serves 2

Ingredients

1 medium aubergine/eggplant

1 large tomato, finely chopped

1 small green and red bell (or pointy) peppers, finely chopped

1 onion, finely chopped

A handful of fresh flat leaf (Italian) parsley, finely chopped

Juice of 1 lemon

30ml/2 tablespoons extra virgin olive oil

10ml/2 teaspoons dried mint

Salt and freshly ground black pepper to taste

This is another delicious salad from Antakya, featuring Turkey's beloved aubergine/eggplant and it is one of my favourites. Aubergine/eggplant here is prepared the same way as in Patlıcanlı Yoğurtlama (see page 87), Smoked aubergine/eggplant with yoghurt, garlic and dried mint, but this time with the addition of other vegetables.

This salad is packed with flavour and is a popular meze on warm summer days. The dried mint really adds a wonderful flavour to the salad, most refreshing along with the lemon juice.

Method

Make sure that you puncture the aubergine/eggplant in 3-4 places before you cook it on a barbecue grill or over a burner. Using a tong, turn occasionally by the stalks until the outer skin is charred and blistered and the inner flesh is soft (if you rather prefer not to have the smoky flavour, the aubergine can be baked in a preheated oven at 200°C/400°F/Gas Mark 6 for about 40 minutes, please turn half way for both sides of the aubergine to cook evenly). Carefully place the cooked aubergine/eggplant in a colander, using a tong. When cool enough to handle, peel away the burnt skin and discard the stalk. Put the flesh in a colander and gently squeeze to drain away any bitter juices. Place the flesh on a chopping board and chop and mash roughly. Transfer the flesh into a plate and pour over ½ lemon juice to retain its colour, mix well. Cover and keep in the fridge until you're ready to make the salad (you can prepare the aubergine/eggplant this way a day in advance if you like).

When you are ready to make the salad, take out the cooked aubergine/eggplant from the fridge.

Rub the onion with a good pinch of salt in a mixing bowl. This softens the onion slightly, making it much more palatable. Add the aubergine flesh to the mixing bowl and stir in the chopped tomatoes, bell peppers and the parsley. Combine all well.

To make the dressing, combine the remaining ½ lemon juice, extra virgin olive oil, dried mint and ground black pepper to taste. Drizzle over the salad, mix well and serve.

Afiyet Olsun.

Smoked aubergine/eggplant salad with garlic yoghurt & dried mint
Patlıcanlı Yoğurtlama

Serves 2

Ingredients

1 medium aubergine/ eggplant

1 garlic clove, finely chopped

240ml/8fl oz plain
(preferably whole milk) yoghurt

5ml/1 teaspoon dried mint

15ml/1 tablespoon
extra virgin olive oil

Juice of ½ lemon

Salt and freshly ground black
pepper to taste

This salad from Antakya in southern Turkey features our beloved patlıcan, aubergine/eggplant. Traditionally, aubergine/eggplant is cooked over an open fire. To get the smoky flavour at home, you can cook the aubergine/eggplant over a burner or on the barbecue. This dish can be served as part of a meze spread or as a side dish with grilled meats and vegetables. The dried mint adds a delicious, refreshing flavour to the salad.

Method

Puncture the aubergine/eggplant in 3-4 places and cook on a barbecue grill or over a burner. Using a tong, turn occasionally by the stalks until the outer skin is charred and blistered and the inner flesh is soft (if you rather prefer not to have the smoky flavour, the aubergine/eggplant can be baked in a preheated oven at 200°C/400°F/Gas Mark 6 for about 40 minutes, please turn half way for both sides of the aubergine/eggplant to cook evenly). Carefully place the cooked aubergine/eggplant in a colander, using a tong. When it is cool enough to handle, peel away the burnt skin and discard the stalk. Put the flesh in a colander and gently squeeze to drain away any bitter juices. Place the flesh on a chopping board and chop and mash roughly. Transfer the flesh into a plate and pour lemon juice over to retain its colour, mix well. Cover and keep in the fridge until you're ready to make the salad (you can prepare the aubergine/eggplant this way a day in advance if you like).

When you are ready to make the salad, take out the cooked aubergine/ eggplant from the fridge. Combine the cooked aubergine/eggplant flesh with yoghurt, garlic, salt, ground black pepper and the dried mint in a mixing bowl. Transfer the mixture to a serving dish, sprinkle a little more dried mint and drizzle the extra virgin olive oil over. Serve as part of the meze spread or as an accompaniment to grills and kebabs.

Afiyet Olsun.

Shepherd's salad with sumac
Sumaklı Çoban Salata

Serves 4

Ingredients

Half of a large cucumber, about 160g/5½oz, cut in quarters and chopped in thin slices

3 medium tomatoes, coarsely chopped

3 spring onions/scallions finely chopped

Handful of flat leaf (Italian) parsley, coarsely chopped

30ml/2 tablespoons extra virgin olive oil

Juice of ½ lemon

5 ml/1 teaspoon ground sumac

Salt and ground black pepper to taste

Shepherd's salad, Çoban Salata is one of the most popular salads in Turkish cuisine. It works well with many meat, fish and vegetable courses. Or have it for lunch with cheese and crusty bread. Chopped onions and pointy green peppers, sivri biber can be added to give this salad extra texture. The traditional Turkish salad dressing of olive oil and lemon juice works well in Çoban Salata. I also like to add a pinch of sumac for extra tanginess and zing.

Method

Combine the cucumbers, tomatoes, spring onions/scallions and the parsley in a bowl. Stir in the olive oil and lemon juice.

Season with salt and ground black pepper. Sprinkle sumac and mix well.

Afiyet Olsun.

Turkish bean salad with olives & eggs
Fasülye Piyazı

Serves 4

Ingredients

2x400g/2x14oz cans of precooked cannellini beans

½ red onion, halved and thinly sliced

3 medium tomatoes, roughly chopped

45ml/3 tablespoons Turkish, Greek or Italian olives, halved and stones removed

2 hardboiled eggs, quartered

Small bunch of flat leaf (Italian) parsley, chopped

30ml/2 tablespoons extra virgin olive oil

Juice of 1 lemon

Pinch of red pepper flakes or paprika flakes (optional)

Salt and freshly ground black pepper to taste

Fasülye Piyazı is a tasty, nourishing salad and the traditional accompaniment to Turkish meatballs, köfte. At home, I often have this salad as a meal by itself – the boiled eggs and beans are filling and healthy. Enjoy this easy salad for lunch or serve it with grills.

Note: If you prefer to use the dried beans, you need to soak them in cold water overnight. Then drain the beans and put them in a pan with plenty of fresh water. Cook for about 60 minutes or until tender, adding salt toward the end of the cooking time. Drain and set aside in a bowl, to be used in this salad.

Method

In a mixing bowl, rub a pinch of salt into the onion slices with your hands really well. This will soften the onions and make them more palatable.

Place the precooked beans on a colander, drain its liquid and rinse over running water. Combine the beans with the onions in the mixing bowl.

Stir in the chopped tomatoes, olives, parsley and red pepper or paprika flakes (if used) into the bowl. Pour in the lemon juice and the extra virgin olive oil. Check the seasoning and add salt and ground black pepper to your taste and combine well.

Transfer the salad into a serving plate, decorate with the hard boiled eggs and serve.

Afiyet Olsun.

Gavurdağı salad with pomegranate molasses

Serves 2

Ingredients

3 medium tomatoes, finely chopped

¼ onion, finely chopped

Handful of flat leaf (Italian) parsley, finely chopped

About 60g/2oz walnuts, chopped (about pea size each)

15ml/1 tablespoon extra virgin olive oil

30ml/2 tablespoons pomegranate molasses, nar ekşisi

5ml/1 teaspoon red pepper, paprika or chili flakes

5ml/1 teaspoon sumac (optional)

Salt and ground black pepper to taste

Gavurdağı salad is a tomato-based salad enjoyed throughout Turkey. Named after the Gavur mountains in southeast Turkey, this refreshing salad is from the Gaziantep region where many delicious and spicy dishes come from. I adore the combination of sweet, juicy tomatoes with crunchy walnuts in this salad; the tangy pomegranate molasses, nar ekşisi, complements this salad beautifully too. Gavurdağı salad is served as part of a meze spread at kebab houses in Turkey. You can also enjoy this simple salad for lunch with your favourite cheese, olives or hummus on the side.

Method

In a large bowl, rub the chopped onions with salt, sumac (if using), red pepper flakes and ground black pepper. This will soften the onion and enable the spices to blend in well.

Add the tomatoes, parsley and walnuts to the onions. Then stir in the pomegranate molasses and the extra virgin olive oil and give them a good (but gentle) mix.

Serve as part of your meze spread or as a delicious lunch with hummus, cheese and olives by the side.

Afiyet Olsun.

Radish salad with tahini sauce
Tahinli Turp Salatası

Serves 2-4

Ingredients

200g/7oz red radishes, washed and pat dried

1 clove of garlic, crushed with salt and finely chopped

Juice of 1 small lemon

15ml/1 tablespoon tahini

30ml/2 tablespoons extra virgin olive oil

5ml/1 teaspoon ground cumin

5ml/1 teaspoon red pepper flakes, paprika or chili flakes

Salt and freshly ground black pepper to taste

Sprigs of flat leaf (Italian) parsley to decorate

Juicy and crunchy red radishes, "turp" as we call them in Turkey, add a colourful and delightful peppery taste to dips and salads. In the Adana and Antakya regions of southern Turkey, locals make this radish salad with a simple tahini sauce. I like to serve this Tahinli Turp Salatası as part of a meze spread. It also accompanies the nutty, grainy Oruk, our version of the Middle Eastern kibbeh well.

Method

Clean and pat dry the radishes. Trim off the stem end and tip, keep the skin.

Grate the radishes coarsely and place in a bowl. Sprinkle some salt over and let the moisture come out, for 5 minutes. Using an absorbent kitchen paper towel or clean tea towel, squeeze the grated radishes to get rid of the excess moisture. Then place them in a serving bowl.

To make the tahini sauce; combine the tahini, chopped garlic, lemon juice and extra virgin olive oil in a small container and mix well. Season with salt and freshly ground black pepper to your taste.

Pour in this sauce over the grated radishes and combine well.

Sprinkle the ground cumin and red pepper flakes over the radish salad and decorate with sprigs of flat leaf parsley.

Afiyet Olsun.

Watercress salad with walnuts and pomegranates

Serves 3-4

Ingredients

3 medium tomatoes, finely chopped

200g/7oz watercress, washed and pat dried with paper towel

¼ onion, finely chopped

Handful of flat leaf (Italian) parsley, finely chopped

60g/2oz walnuts, chopped (about pea size each)

15ml/1 tablespoon extra virgin olive oil

30ml/2 tablespoons pomegranate molasses

5ml/1 teaspoon red pepper flakes, paprika or chili flakes

5ml/1 teaspoon sumac (optional)

Salt and ground black pepper to taste

90g/3oz pomegranate seeds to serve

Inspired by the Gavurdağı salad, we made a variation with this watercress salad at one of my Turkish cookery classes. Adding watercress and pomegranate seeds to the salad turned out to be a great success and gave the salad an extra freshness with the pomegranate seeds. It was a big hit with the class and is an impressive salad for easy entertaining.

Method

In a large bowl, rub the chopped onions with salt, sumac, red pepper flakes and ground black pepper. This will soften the onion and enable the spices to blend in well.

Add the watercress, tomatoes, parsley and walnuts to the onions. Combine well.

Then stir in the pomegranate molasses and the extra virgin olive oil and give them a good, but gentle mix. Sprinkle pomegranate seeds over the salad and serve.

Afiyet Olsun.

Purslane salad with garlic yoghurt
Yoğurtlu Semizotu Salatası

Serves 2

Ingredients

*90g/3oz fresh purslane leaves,
washed and pat dried*

*240ml/8fl oz plain
(preferably whole milk) yoghurt*

*1 garlic clove,
crushed and finely chopped*

Pinch of salt

5ml/1 teaspoon dried mint

*10ml/2 teaspoons
extra virgin olive oil*

Ground black pepper to taste

*Red pepper flakes, chili or paprika
flakes to sprinkle*

This versatile salad is easy to make and can be served as an appetizer, meze or a side dish with grilled meats, poultry and pasta. Often cooked in Turkish homes, this salad is also served as part of a meze spread with warm pide bread in restaurants and kebab houses. It also makes a wonderful and healthy lunch alternative. Watercress or lamb's lettuce can be used as a substitute for purslane.

Method

Crush and finely chop the garlic. Rub a little salt to the garlic; that will soften the garlic and release its oils. In a wide bowl, beat the yoghurt with the garlic. Season with ground black pepper.

Combine purslane into the bowl, add the dried mint and mix well. Transfer into a serving plate and sprinkle a few red pepper flakes over. Drizzle extra virgin olive oil over the salad and serve immediately.

Afiyet Olsun.

Chapter Five

Turkish Breakfast

Turkish Breakfast

For many Turks a hearty breakfast, kahvaltı, is their favourite meal of the day. It is mine also. Therefore, I feel breakfast deserves a chapter of its own. Turks love a good, unrushed breakfast with family and friends, especially at the weekends. A typical Turkish breakfast is a palette of tastes featuring eggs prepared several ways, olives, a variety of cheeses, sliced cucumbers, tomatoes and pointy peppers, gözleme, pide bread, honey with thick Turkish clotted cream, kaymak, variety of jams, seasonal fruit and many more. Gözleme is a stuffed Anatolian flat bread with a variety of fillings. It is a popular street food baked fresh in markets and gözleme stalls throughout Turkey.

Paying homage to my family's southern Turkish roots, breakfast at my parents includes regional specialities such as the Olive salad with pomegranate molasses and za'atar – Zeytin Üfeleme and Crumbled feta salad flavoured with cumin, za'atar and red pepper flakes - Çökelek Salata. Enjoyed with endless glasses of çay (Turkish tea), Turkish breakfast is the feast I miss and long for, and I am eager to recreate wherever I am. I hope it inspires you to enjoy with family and friends too.

Olive salad with pomegranate molasses and za'atar
Zeytin Üfeleme

Serves 2-4

Ingredients

2 spring onions/scallions, finely chopped

A handful of flat leaf parsley, finely chopped

30ml/2 tablespoons fresh za'atar, chopped (if available) OR 15ml/1 tablespoon dried za'atar blend

120ml/4fl oz Turkish or Greek green and black olives, pitted

3 medium tomatoes, finely diced

30ml/2 tablespoons extra virgin olive oil

15ml/1 tablespoon pomegranate molasses, nar ekşisi

Salt and ground black pepper to taste

Wedges of Turkish pide ekmek or pita bread to serve

We Turks love olives. A typical Turkish breakfast starts with a plate of olives, white cheese (beyaz peynir), sliced tomato, cucumber and bread, ekmek on the side. Blessed with a hot dry climate, olive trees grow throughout the Aegean and Mediterranean and the olives are absolutely packed with flavour. I grew up enjoying Zeytin Üfeleme almost daily and I often make this simple and refreshing olive salad for weekend brunch. It features two regional ingredients from Antakya – pomegranate molasses, nar ekşisi for the dressing and the fresh herb, za'atar or the dried za'atar blend is sprinkled over the top. With the recipes in this book, you will soon be able to prepare your own homemade version for pomegranate molasses (page 37) and za'atar blend (page 39).

Method

Place the chopped spring onions/scallions in a bowl and sprinkle a little salt. Rub the salt into the spring onions/scallions with your hands – this will soften the onions and make it more palatable. Stir in the olives, tomatoes and parsley.

Drizzle the extra virgin olive oil and the pomegranate molasses. Stir in the za'atar, season with salt and ground black pepper to taste. Combine thoroughly.

Serve with slices of pide ekmek or pita bread by the side.

Afiyet Olsun.

Crumbled feta salad with cumin and red pepper flakes
Çökelek Salata

Serves 2

Ingredients

½ small red onion, finely diced

2 spring onions/scallions, finely chopped

2 medium tomatoes, finely diced

¼ of large cucumber, finely diced

Handful of flat leaf (Italian) parsley, roughly chopped

110g/4oz Turkish white cheese or feta cheese, crumbled

5ml/1 teaspoon ground cumin

5ml/1 teaspoon red pepper (or paprika) flakes

5ml/1 teaspoon dried oregano

5ml/1 teaspoon ground sumac – optional

30ml/2 tablespoons extra virgin olive oil

15ml/1 tablespoon lemon juice

Salt and ground black pepper to taste

Turkish flat bread or pita bread wedges to serve

This light and healthy salad is a delicious choice for lunch or a weekend brunch. Antakya has a special dried cheese blend with spices called kuru çökelek (also known as sürk), that is traditionally used in this salad. Cumin, red pepper flakes and oregano is mixed in kuru çökelek and is readily available there. If kuru çökelek isn't available, the Turkish white cheese or feta will work just as well. Cumin and red pepper flakes amazingly transform the delicate flavour of white cheese (or feta cheese) to a whole new level.

Method

In a bowl, mix the Turkish white cheese or feta cheese, onion, spring onion/scallion, cumin, oregano and red pepper flakes with your hands. This will soften the onions and infuse the spices to the cheese and onions. Add the tomatoes, cucumber, parsley, olive oil and lemon juice, and mix well. Check the seasoning and add salt and ground black pepper to your taste and sprinkle some sumac over before you serve, if you like.

Serve with Turkish flat bread, pide ekmek or pita bread wedges.

Afiyet Olsun.

Homemade Turkish flat bread with sesame seeds
Pide Ekmek

Serves 8-10

Ingredients

450g/1lb all-purpose/plain flour

7g/1 sachet dried yeast

½ teaspoon sugar

175ml/6fl oz lukewarm water

5ml/1 teaspoon salt

30ml/2 tablespoons whole milk yoghurt

30ml/2 tablespoons olive oil

1 egg, beaten

30ml/2 tablespoons nigella seeds or poppy seeds

30ml/2 tablespoons sesame seeds

Bread, ekmek is a major staple in Turkish cuisine and is served with every meal. My father loves fresh (taze) ekmek and will even have a slice with pasta. Bread is rarely wasted in Turkey; stale bread is used in soups and spreads like walnuts and red pepper paste dip and in desserts. Oval or round pide ekmek is a national favourite and is traditionally cooked in a hot clay oven. Pide bread also plays an important rôle during Ramadan when it is used to break the fast. I have many fond childhood memories strolling through Uzun Çarşı, Long Market in Antakya to buy freshly baked bread; my grandmother would always order an extra as she knew how much we loved pide ekmek and half would be eaten on the way home from the market – too hard to resist!

This pide ekmek recipe is adapted from Ghillie Başan's Classic Turkish Cookery book. It has a crispy crust and a light doughy middle – perfect with mezes, breakfast and casseroles to dip in the juices.

Method

Preheat oven to 200°C/400°F/Gas Mark 6

Cream the yeast with sugar in half of the lukewarm water, leave to froth.

Sift the flour with the salt. Make a well in the middle and pour in the yeast, olive oil, yoghurt and the rest of the water. Using your hands, draw in the flour from the sides and work the mixture into a sticky dough. Add a little more water if necessary. Knead until the dough is smooth and leaves the sides of the bowl (drizzle a little oil in your hands to help shape the dough, if needed).

Continue to knead on a lightly floured surface until the dough is elastic and smooth. Roll it in the few drops of olive oil in the bowl, cover it with a damp tea towel and leave to prove in a warm place for 1 hour or until doubled in size.

Once doubled, punch the dough down, knead again and divide it into two pieces. Knead each piece well. Flatten them out with the heel of your hand and stretch them into large, uneven rounds or ovals, creating a thick lip around the edges. Indent the dough with your fingertips.

Preheat 2 trays with baking/parchment sheets in the oven for 2 minutes. Place the pide breads on them and brush the pides with the beaten egg. Then sprinkle the nigella (or poppy) seeds and sesame seeds over the top.

Bake the pides for 18–20 minutes, until lightly golden with a crisp crust around the edges.

Once baked, transfer them to a wire rack. If you want them to retain their softness, wrap them in aluminium foil or in a dry towel while still warm.

Afiyet Olsun.

Tahini bread with sesame and nigella seeds
Tahinli Ekmek

Serves 4-6

Ingredients

For the dough:

450g/1lb all-purpose/plain flour

7g/1 sachet of dried yeast

5g/1 teaspoon salt

½ teaspoon sugar

240ml/8fl oz warm water

45ml/3 tablespoons mild olive oil

For the filling and decoration:

30ml/2 tablespoons tahini

15ml/1 tablespoon nigella seeds

15ml/1 tablespoon sesame seeds

30ml/2 tablespoons mild olive oil

This tahini bread recipe comes from Antakya. Tahini is a thick, smooth paste made from ground sesame seeds. It has a rich, nutty flavour and is commonly used in southern Turkish cuisine. Tahini is a popular ingredient in dips (such as hummus), salads, and is often used in baking. Nothing beats the early morning aromas of freshly baked tahini breads from the local bakeries in Antakya. Try tahini bread rolls with dips, cheese or salads.

Method

Preheat oven to 180°C/350°F/Gas Mark 4

In a large bowl, combine the flour, salt, sugar and yeast. Stir in the olive oil. Add warm water and mix to form a soft dough. Knead for 5 minutes on a floured surface or until the dough is smooth and elastic. Shape as a ball and place on a large, oiled bowl. Cover the dough with cling film/plastic wrap or a damp tea towel and leave to rise in a warm place for about 45 minutes or until double in size.

Generously oil a baking tray. Take about a tennis ball size dough and roll out the ball to make a small oval shape, about 15cm/6in long. Spread a generous teaspoon of tahini in the middle of the dough and roll like a cigar. Then swirl to make a spiral. Place the finished roll on the greased tray and decorate with a sprinkle of sesame and nigella seeds. Tap the top of the dough gently for the seeds to settle. Repeat these steps for the rest of the dough.

Place the tray in the centre rack of the preheated oven and bake for 30-35 minutes until the top of the rolls start to get a golden colour.

Serve the rolls warm with dips like walnut red pepper paste spread, hummus or soups. They are also lovely to dip into olive oil then to za'atar blend, as the locals would do for breakfast.

Afiyet Olsun.

Anatolian flat breads with spinach and cheese
Ispanaklı, Peynirli Gözleme

Makes 5 gözleme

Ingredients

450g/1lb all-purpose/plain flour

7g/1 sachet instant dried yeast

Pinch of salt

45ml/3 tablespoons olive oil

30ml/2 tablespoons plain yoghurt (preferably whole milk)

270ml/9fl oz warm water (150ml/5fl oz warm water to be mixed with the yeast)

For the filling:

200g/7oz baby spinach leaves

1 onion, finely chopped

5ml/1 teaspoon Turkish red pepper flakes or chili flakes

230g/8oz feta cheese

15ml/1 tablespoon olive oil

These delicious stuffed flat breads are made with a variety of fillings. My favourites are spinach with cheese, and minced/ground meat with onions. Gözleme is cooked on a hot griddle and being a popular street food, there are always gözleme stalls in markets and cafes. Enjoy gözleme with a glass of Turkish tea, çay, or our traditional yoghurt drink, ayran.

This recipe is for dear David and Claire, for their love of Turkish cuisine.

Method

Combine about 150ml/ 5fl oz warm water, yeast and a pinch of salt in a small bowl and stir to dissolve. Stand it in a warm place for 5 minutes or until bubbles form on the surface.

Sift the flour into a large bowl. Make a well in the middle and pour in the yeast, water and salt mixture, olive oil, yoghurt and the remaining warm water. Using your hand, draw in the flour from the sides and work the mixture into a dough. Knead thoroughly to form a soft dough. If it gets sticky, have a little olive oil in your hands to shape the dough. Divide the dough into 5 pieces, knead and roll into balls. Place the balls on a floured surface, cover with a damp cloth and leave to rest for 1 hour, or until the dough is doubled in size.

Meanwhile, prepare the filling. Chop the washed spinach leaves roughly. Knead the onions, spinach, olive oil and red pepper flakes for a few minutes. Stir in the feta cheese and combine well.

On a lightly floured surface, roll out each of the balls of the dough with a rolling pin into thin, flat rounds, about 40cm/16in diameter. Sprinkle a little flour as you roll the dough so that the dough won't stick. Roll until you achieve a thin sheet of a flat round.

Fold the top and bottom sides of the dough in a way for the edges to meet in the middle. Spread about 2 ½ tablespoons filling into the middle part of this flat sheet. Then fold the right and left edges over the filling, making sure all the filling is safely covered. Press the edges together well to seal. Repeat the same procedure for the rest of the dough balls.

Heat a griddle or a non-stick pan, and brush one side of the gözleme with a little olive oil and place on the pan to cook for about 2-3 minutes, or until golden brown. Brush the uncooked side with a little olive oil and then flip it over. Cook for another 2-3 minutes, until golden brown. Cook the rest of the gözleme the same way.

Brush both cooked sides of the gözleme with a little olive oil - this will keep the gözleme moist. You can either roll the gözleme to serve, or you can cut in halves or quarters.

Afiyet Olsun.

Turkish style scrambled eggs with peppers, tomatoes and onions
Menemen

Serves 4-6

Ingredients

8 eggs

1 green bell pepper or 2 pointy green peppers, sivri biber, finely sliced

3 spring onions/scallions, finely sliced

4 medium ripe tomatoes, finely diced

15ml/1 tablespoon olive oil

15ml/1 tablespoon butter

120g/4oz Turkish white cheese or feta cheese, crumbled

5-10ml/1-2 teaspoons Turkish red pepper flakes or chili flakes

Salt and ground black pepper to taste

Crusty bread or wedges of pide or pita bread to serve

Menemen is a Turkish style scrambled eggs with vegetables and it is my husband's favourite. Popular in many Turkish households as a weekend breakfast, Turkish white cheese, beyaz peynir, is often added. Ripe, juicy tomatoes add colour and sweetness. Traditionally Turkish green pointy peppers, sivri biber, are used but green bell peppers also work well in the recipe. Served with crusty bread, Menemen also makes a satisfying lunch or light supper option.

Method

Crack the eggs in a bowl and mix. Add the Turkish white cheese or feta cheese, combine well.

Heat the butter and the olive oil in a large frying pan. Stir in the green bell peppers or pointy peppers, sivri biber and cook for a couple of minutes, at a low to medium heat. Add the spring onions/scallions, tomatoes and red pepper flakes, mix well. Pour in the egg mixture into the frying pan and give it a good stir. Scramble the eggs over a medium heat until they are just done, retaining their juice. Season with salt and ground black pepper to taste.

Serve with crusty bread or with wedges of pide or pita bread.

Afiyet Olsun.

Eggs with spicy Turkish sausage
Sucuklu Yumurta

Serves 2

Ingredients

*115g/4oz Turkish sucuk
(or any other dried sausage
of your choice), sliced*

2-4 medium free range eggs

30ml/2 tablespoons olive oil

5ml/1 teaspoon ground cumin

*5ml/1 teaspoon red pepper
(or paprika) flakes*

*Salt and ground black pepper
to taste*

*Crusty bread or wedges of pide
or pita bread to serve*

Sucuklu Yumurta is another favourite Turkish breakfast. Shaped like a horseshoe, sucuk is a dried cured sausage made with lamb or beef and flavoured with garlic, cumin and red pepper flakes. In rural areas, people make their own sucuk with a variety of spices and hang them outside their homes to cure. Turkish and Middle Eastern markets stock sucuk but if you can't find them, any other dried cured sausages are a good substitute.

Method

Heat the oil in the frying pan. Stir in the sliced sucuk (or your choice of dried sausage) and sauté over a medium heat for a minute or two until they start to brown. Scatter the sausages around the edges of the pan forming a circle. Crack the eggs in the middle and cook for a few minutes on medium heat. Season with salt and ground black pepper and sprinkle ground cumin and red pepper flakes over the eggs, if you like. Cook until the egg whites are set and the egg yolks are still runny.

Serve with crusty bread or with wedges of pide or pita bread.

Afiyet Olsun.

Eggs with spinach and onions
Ispanaklı Yumurta

Serves 2

Ingredients

400g/14oz fresh spinach leaves, washed

1 small onion, finely chopped

2 medium eggs

30ml/2 tablespoons olive oil

Salt and ground black pepper to taste

½ teaspoon cumin – optional

½ teaspoon red pepper flakes – optional

A dollop of plain yoghurt to serve

Crusty bread or wedges of pide or pita bread to serve

This versatile egg recipe can be served for breakfast, brunch or lunch. My children like this dish as a weekend breakfast or light supper. A serving of plain yoghurt on the side complements Ispanaklı Yumurta well. Make sure to have some crusty bread, Turkish pide ekmek or pita wedges to soak up the delicious juices.

Method

Heat the olive oil in a shallow pan and sauté the onions for 3 minutes, until they are softened. Add the spinach and let it wilt gently for 1-2 minutes, giving a gentle stir. Season with salt and ground black pepper.

Make two hollows in the spinach mixture and crack the eggs. Cook over a medium to low heat until the whites are firm but the yolks remain soft. Season with salt and ground black pepper. Sprinkle ground cumin and red pepper flakes over the eggs (if you are using them).

Serve immediately with crusty bread, pide bread or pita wedges. A splash of plain yoghurt by the side complements this dish well.

Afiyet Olsun.

Chapter Six

Savoury Pastries & Flat Breads

Savoury pastries

Savoury pastries are an indispensable part of Turkish cuisine and I have a soft spot for them. The most popular - and my favourite - are börek, gözleme and pides. Börek is a versatile little pastry with filling, enjoyed with breakfast, as a mid-day snack with a glass of Turkish tea, çay or served in a meze spread. There is Börekçi (Börek shop) in every neighbourhood at home. Traditionally made with fresh yufka (similar to filo) sheets, böreks are also a special part of ladies' afternoon tea gatherings. My mother would bake at least two varieties of börek when we had visitors and I would always look forward to this feast as a child.

Pide is an oval flat bread with toppings and another savoury delight we Turks love. Like Börekçi there seems to be a pide shop on every street corner in Istanbul. It is a perfect and speedy snack food with a wide variety of toppings from pastırma (Turkish dried cured beef), to cheese, peppers and tomatoes. This chapter also includes some southern Turkish savoury specialities like flat bread with za'atar, feta and pepper paste, Biberli Ekmek.

Savoury pastries are always well-liked at my Turkish cookery classes. Everyone is surprised at how simple they are to make. Fresh yufka sheets are difficult to find in ordinary grocery stores abroad, so I substitute filo pastry sheets for yufka in my börek recipes, which works just as well. I hope you enjoy creating your own savoury pastries with these recipes.

Tray bake spinach and cheese filo pastry
Ispanaklı, Peynirli Börek

Serves 8

Ingredients

24 sheets of filo pastry – 48cm x 25cm/19in x 10in each sheet, thawed

200g/7oz spinach leaves, washed and pat dried

200g/7oz Turkish white cheese or feta cheese, juice drained and mashed with a fork

110g/4oz grated mozzarella

3 eggs, beaten

120ml/4fl oz milk

120ml/4fl oz water

45ml/3 tablespoons mild olive oil

30ml/2 tablespoons sesame seeds

This börek is immensely popular throughout my homeland as well as at my Turkish cookery classes. It is also my children's favourite snack food - even the fussiest child will enjoy this börek and ask for seconds. I use filo pastry and you'll be amazed how simple it is to make.

Turkish white cheese, beyaz peynir is traditionally used in this börek. Living abroad, it's hard to get beyaz peynir so I use a combination of feta cheese and grated mozzarella, which work well. Serve this flavourful vegetarian börek for brunch or for lunch with a light salad or as an appetizer for a dinner party.

Method

Preheat oven to 180°C/350°F/Gas Mark 4

Wash the spinach leaves, pat dry and chop roughly. Beat 2 eggs in a small bowl.

Combine the Turkish white cheese or feta cheese, grated mozzarella and two beaten eggs with the spinach leaves in a large bowl. In a separate bowl, mix the water, 1 tablespoon of olive oil and milk.

Grease the baking tray with the remaining olive oil. Lay the pastry sheets alongside the baking tray. Open the filo sheets only when you are ready to use them and cover the rest with a slightly damp towel so that they don't dry out.

Lay two filo sheets in the greased baking tray. Pour 2 tablespoons of the milk-olive oil-water mixture and brush all over the sheet. Repeat this layering until you reach the 12th sheet, using two filo sheets each time.

When you reached the 12th filo sheet, spread the spinach and cheese filling evenly. Continue layering the filo sheets and spreading over the milk mixture every two layers until you reach the 24th sheet.

Beat the remaining egg with a drop of olive oil and brush over the final sheet. Sprinkle sesame seeds all over the pastry.

Bake the börek in the preheated oven 180°C/350°F/Gas Mark 4 for about 30-35 minutes, until the top is golden brown. Take the börek out of the oven and cover with flax or parchment/baking paper for 10 minutes, this will keep the börek moist.

Cut into pieces and serve warm or at room temperature.

Tips: 1) This börek freezes wonderfully. Once cooled, slice the börek and put in freezer bags and seal to freeze. You can reheat the frozen börek in a greased tray at a preheated oven at 180°C/350°F/Gas Mark 4 for about 10 minutes. 2) You can also use your favourite cheese, mashed potato, grated courgette/zucchini as well as herbs like parsley and dill as part of the filling.

Afiyet Olsun.

Tray bake filo pastry with minced/ground meat
Kıymalı Tepsi Böreği

Serves 8
Ingredients

24 sheets of filo pastry – 48cm x 25cm/19in x 10in each, thawed

2 onions, finely chopped

400g/14oz minced/ground beef or lamb (or a mixture)

2 eggs

120ml/4fl oz whole milk

Extra 30ml/2 tablespoons whole milk for the top of the pastry

120ml/4fl oz water

45ml/3 tablespoons olive oil

Salt and freshly ground black pepper to taste

Minced/ground meat (beef or lamb) cooked with onion works so well as a filling for this Kıymalı Tepsi Böreği and it is easy to make. Yufka is fresh Turkish pastry sheets used at home to make this börek, which is baked in a round tray called tepsi. My mother would prepare this börek as an after-school snack when I was a child; coming home to the aromas of this freshly cooked börek was always heavenly. I use filo pastry sheets as an alternative to yufka and they work just as well. Enjoy this börek as an appetizer or with tea for a quick morning or afternoon snack.

Method

Preheat oven to 180°C/350°F/Gas Mark 4

Heat 15ml/1 tablespoon olive oil in a wide, heavy pan and stir in the chopped onions. Sauté over medium heat for 3 minutes to soften them up.

Stir in the minced/ground meat to the onion mixture and sauté for another 5 minutes over a medium heat. Season with salt and freshly ground black pepper, the filling is ready. Turn the heat off and leave it aside to cool.

Beat 1 egg and 1 egg white (save the remaining 1 egg yolk in a small bowl for later) and combine with milk and water in a bowl. Grease the baking tray with 15ml/1 tablespoon of olive oil.

Lay the pastry sheets alongside the baking tray. Open the filo sheets only when you are ready to use them and cover the rest with a slightly damp towel so that they don't dry out.

Lay two filo sheets in the greased baking tray. Pour 2 tablespoons of the milk mixture and brush all over the sheet. Repeat this layering until you reach the 12th sheet, using two filo sheets each time.

Once you have reached the 12th sheet, spread the minced meat and onion mixture evenly over the pastry. Continue layering the filo sheets and spreading over the milk mixture every two layers until you reach the 24th sheet.

Combine the extra 30ml/2 tablespoons milk with the remaining egg yolk and 15ml/1 tablespoon olive oil. Brush this mixture over the last sheet of the filo pastry.

Bake in the pre-heated oven at 180°C/350°F/Gas Mark 4 for 30-35 minutes, until the top of the pastry turns to golden to light brown.

Once cooked, cover with a baking/parchment paper to keep moist and cool for 10 minutes. Slice into squares and serve them warm. You'll have the children, and the adults, coming back for more – everytime.

Afiyet Olsun.

Baked spinach and cheese filo triangles
Muska Böreği

Serves 6-8

Ingredients

12 sheets of filo pastry - 48cm x 25cm/19 x 10in each, thawed

150g/5½ oz spinach leaves

150g/5½ oz feta cheese, mashed with a fork

110g/4oz grated mozzarella

3 eggs, beaten

45ml/3 tablespoons mild olive oil

Small bowl of water to seal the pastry

These small triangle-shaped pastries, muska böreği, are delightful and perfect for entertaining. They are traditionally made with fresh Turkish yufka pastry sheets. I substitute with filo pastry sheets and it works just as well. Turkish white cheese called beyaz peynir, is traditionally used in these pastries. The closest I can find outside Turkey is feta cheese. It is drier so I add a little grated mozzarella with the feta for a creamier consistency and to balance the flavours. Chopped parsley is a good alternative to spinach in the filling.

Method

Preheat oven to 180°C/350°F/Gas Mark 4

Remove the stalks of the spinach, wash and chop roughly. In a large bowl, combine the spinach with the feta cheese, grated mozzarella, 1 tablespoon of olive oil and two of the beaten eggs. The filling is now ready.

In a separate bowl, mix 1 egg and 2 tablespoons of olive oil. Also grease a baking tray with a little olive oil.

Lay the pastry sheets on a clean surface and cut into 10cm x 25cm/4in x 10in strips. Stack the strips on top of one another and cover with a damp towel so that they won't dry out. Keep a bowl of water near you.

Lay two strips of filo sheets on top of one another. Place 15ml/1 tablespoon of the spinach and cheese mixture at the end of the filo pastry strip near you. Fold the end of the strip over the filling diagonally so that it forms a triangle. Continue folding the strip in triangles until you get a small, triangular stuffed pastry.

Seal the pastry with the water; water really helps to keep filo sheets intact here. Repeat with remaining filo until you have used all of the filling.

Place the stuffed triangle pastries seam side down on the greased baking dish. Brush them with the egg and olive oil mixture. Bake the triangles in the oven for about 20–25 minutes, until they are golden brown. Serve hot as an appetizer or as part of a meze spread.

Afiyet Olsun.

Savoury pastry with cheese and parsley
Peynirli Poğaça

Makes 11 Poğaças

Ingredients

For the dough:

7g/1 sachet dried yeast

425g/15oz all-purpose plain flour

5ml/1 teaspoon salt

90ml/3fl oz plain (whole milk) yoghurt

1 egg, beaten

120ml/4fl oz mild olive oil or sunflower oil

120ml/4fl oz warm milk

For the filling:

170g/6oz Turkish white cheese, beyaz peynir or feta cheese, crumbled

15g/0.4oz flat leaf (Italian) parsley, finely chopped

For the topping:

1 egg, beaten

Sesame seeds and nigella seeds to decorate

Poğaça is a popular savoury pastry throughout the Balkans as well as in Turkey. They are traditionally an oval shaped pastry with fillings and popular for breakfast or as a snack with tea back home. Local bakeries and street stalls sell freshly baked poğaças with a variety of fillings using white cheese, olives or potatoes; we Turks love them. With a glass of çay, tea by the side, they make a delicious and affordable breakfast or teatime treat.

Method

Preheat the oven to 180°C/ 350°F/Gas Mark 4

Combine the warm milk and dried yeast in a small bowl and mix well. Let it stand for 5 minutes so that it gets foamy.

In a large bowl, stir in the flour and salt and make a well in the middle. Add the yoghurt, mild olive oil (or sunflower oil) and the beaten egg to the flour mixture. Stir in the foamy yeast mixture and knead well with your hands for a few minutes, until you have a smooth dough. Shape the dough like a ball, place in the large bowl and cover with cling film/plastic wrap. Let it rise in a warm place for 45-60 minutes or until doubled in size.

While the dough is rising, prepare your filling. In a medium size bowl, stir in the crumbled Turkish white cheese or feta cheese and chopped parsley. Combine well.

Once the dough has risen, punch down and divide into 11 equal pieces, each about a size of a small tangerine. Roll each piece into a ball, and then press to flatten into a round flat circle with your fingertips, about 10cm/4in in diameter (you can make them smaller if you prefer). Place a spoonful of the filling mixture (take care not to overfill) at one side of the dough circle, leaving a little unfilled dough margin near the edges. Fold the circle to cover the filling to form a half-moon shape. Make sure the dough covers the filling and meet the other end. Seal the two ends of the dough by pressing with your fingertips. Place the stuffed dough on the greased tray and repeat this procedure with the rest of the dough pieces.

Place all the prepared poğaças side-by-side on a greased tray. Brush them with the beaten egg and sprinkle with nigella and sesame seeds. Bake in the preheated oven 180°C/350°F/Gas Mark 4 on the middle rack for about 25–30 minutes, until they are golden brown on top.

Serve warm; a glass of çay, Turkish tea goes really well with these delicious poğaças.

Afiyet Olsun.

135

Antakya style flat breads with feta, za'tar and red pepper paste
Biberli Ekmek

Serves 8

Ingredients

For the dough:

450g/1lb all-purpose/plain flour

7g/1 sachet dried yeast

5ml/1 teaspoon salt

120ml/4fl oz lukewarm milk

180ml/6fl oz lukewarm water

90ml/3fl oz olive oil

For the topping:

200g/7oz crumbled feta cheese or çökelek

30ml/2 tablespoons red pepper paste, biber salçası

30ml/2 tablespoons concentrated tomato paste

10ml/2 teaspoons ground cumin

60ml/4 tablespoons sesame seeds

30ml/2 tablespoons zahtar or za'atar blend

45ml/3 tablespoons olive oil

This delicious flat bread with za'atar topping is a speciality from my home town of Antakya and always brings back fond memories. As a youngster, I loved the ritual of preparing the topping and taking it to the local bakery to be baked and with expectation, waiting to pick up our Biberli Ekmek. The baker would always make an extra tiny flat bread with the topping for us to taste - they always smelled mesmerizing and we couldn't wait to have a bite.

You can make your own za'atar blend with my recipe in this book (see page 39). Biberli Ekmek is traditionally made with Antakya's çökelek cheese which is a cross between a mild crumbled feta and a drier form of cottage cheese. Feta cheese will work well. I enjoy this delicious flat bread with a meze spread or just on its own with a cup of tea.

Method

Preheat the oven to 180°C/350°F/Gas Mark 4

Prepare the topping first. Combine the crumbled feta or çökelek, red pepper paste, tomato paste, all the spices, sesame seeds and olive oil. Knead with your hands to blend them well to form a smooth paste. Set the topping aside.

Now make the dough. Combine the flour, dried yeast and salt in a large bowl.

Stir in the warm milk, warm water and olive oil and knead for 3 minutes to form a soft dough. If it gets sticky, drizzle a little more olive oil in your hand to shape the dough, it really helps.

Grease a baking tray with 1 tablespoon of olive oil and spread the dough as a thin flat bread base, reaching all the edges about 0.25cm/0.09in.

Spread the topping evenly as a thin base over the flat bread. Leave the flat bread with topping on at a warm spot to rise for 30 minutes.

Once the dough has risen, bake in the preheated oven 180°C/350°F/Gas Mark 4 for 18-20 minutes.

Let the baked flat bread with topping, Biberli Ekmek to cool down for 15 minutes. Then slice and serve as part of a meze spread or with tea, Turkish çay.

Afiyet Olsun.

Antakya's Kaytaz Böreği with minced/ground meat topping

Serves 6-8

Ingredients

For the dough:

460g/1lb all-purpose/plain flour

7g/1 sachet dried yeast

60ml/4 tablespoons olive oil

5ml/1 teaspoon salt

300ml/10fl oz warm water

For the topping:

225g/8oz minced/ground beef

1 onion, finely grated

30ml/2 tablespoons of double concentrated tomato paste

5ml/1 teaspoon freshly ground black pepper

Salt to taste

60ml/4fl oz olive oil in a bowl to shape

Lemon wedges to serve

Kaytaz böreği is a personal favourite from our home town Antakya; my mother would knock off these delicious börek with such ease when I was a child. The smell of the freshly baked kaytaz börek always warmly greeted us coming home from school.

Kaytaz böreği is made with a light soft dough. My mother describes the dough as having "earlobe consistency" which always makes me smile from ear to ear! This regional speciality from Antakya requires a generous amount of olive oil to stretch and shape each pastry. I like to squeeze a little lemon juice over the cooked pastry to add a sharp citrusy flavor to the meat filling.

Method

Preheat the oven to 180°C/350°F/Gas Mark 4

In a large bowl, combine the flour, salt and yeast and mix well. Stir in the olive oil and warm water and knead into a soft dough (if it's sticky, you may need a little extra flour to shape the dough). Drizzle a little olive oil into your hands and coat the dough with this olive oil. Place the dough in a large bowl and cover with cling film/plastic wrap. Leave it to rest and rise at a warm spot for 45 minutes or until it doubles in size.

While the dough is resting, prepare the topping. Combine the grated onion, minced/ground beef, tomato paste, season with salt and ground black pepper. Really knead well with your hands, until all the ingredients have combined thoroughly.

Once the dough has risen, divide the dough into small tangerine size pieces. Have the bowl of olive oil near you and brush the surface with a little olive oil. Take a piece of the dough and place it on the oiled surface. Dip your fingers in the olive oil bowl and stretch the dough into a thin square piece with your fingers. Fold the right and left sides then the top and bottom sides of the dough to form a neat square package of 8cm x 8cm, 3in x 3in. Dip your fingers into olive oil again and brush the top of the pastry. Then, place the prepared dough into a well-oiled baking tray. Repeat the same procedure with the remaining dough and place on the baking tray side-by-side, leaving 2cm/0.8in between the dough parcels.

Place a generous tablespoon of topping on each dough parcel and spread and press gently.

Bake in the preheated oven 180°C/350°F/Gas Mark 4 for 20-25 minutes until the top of the pastry turns golden.

Serve warm with wedges of lemon by the side. Kaytaz böreği makes a wonderful starter or lunch and it also goes well as a mid-day snack with a cup of tea, çay.

Afiyet Olsun.

Oval flat breads with cheese, peppers, onion and spinach
Peynirli, Sebzeli Pide

Serves 6-8 (makes 2 pides)

Ingredients

For the dough:

300g/10½oz + 30ml/2 tablespoons all-purpose/plain flour

7g/1 sachet of dried yeast

240ml/8fl oz warm water

45ml/3 tablespoons olive oil

Pinch of salt

For the topping:

1 medium onion, finely chopped

200g/7oz spinach leaves, washed and pat dried

200g/7oz feta cheese, crumbled

1 red bell pepper, de-seeded and cut in half lengthways and thinly sliced

5ml/1 teaspoon red pepper flakes

15ml/1 tablespoon olive oil

Salt and freshly ground black pepper to taste

1 beaten egg + 15ml/1 tablespoon of olive oil to brush the pide

Pide, oval flat breads with toppings, is our popular "fast food" in Turkey. There are pide shops called Pideci that only bake these flat breads and serve them all day long at home.

Pide is made with a wide variety of toppings from vegetables or with meats such as sucuk (Turkish spicy sausage) and pastırma, Turkish dried cured beef. Sometimes an egg can be cracked over pide, as in some examples of Karadeniz Pidesi, from the Black Sea region. Everyone I know loves the topping in this recipe; sautéed onions and pepper add a delicious sweetness.

Method

Preheat the oven to 180°C/ 350°F/Gas Mark 4

Stir in the dried yeast in a small bowl and pour in 120ml/4fl oz warm water. Dissolve the yeast in water, mixing with your fingers. Set aside for the yeast mixture to get frothy for 5 minutes.

Combine the flour and salt in a large bowl. Make a well in the middle and pour in 30ml/2 tablespoons of olive oil and the yeast mixture. Pour in the remaining warm water to the flour mixture. Draw in the flour from the sides and work the mixture into a dough. Knead for 3-5 minutes, until you reach a smooth dough. The dough gets sticky as you knead, so pour the remaining 15ml/1 tablespoon of olive oil and stir in additional 30ml/2 tablespoons of flour to help shape into a soft dough.

Place the dough in large bowl and cover with cling film/plastic wrap. Leave it in a warm place for 1 hour to double in size.

For the topping; heat 15ml/1 tablespoon of olive oil in a wide heavy pan and stir in the onions and peppers. Sauté for 3-5 minutes over a medium heat. Turn the heat off and stir in the spinach, red pepper flakes and crumbled feta cheese, combine well. Season with salt and freshly ground black pepper.

Once the dough has risen, place the dough on a lightly floured surface. Knead the dough for a minute then divide into two pieces and roll into two balls. On a lightly floured surface, roll the dough balls into 2 oval shapes of 20cm x 40cm/ about 8in x16in, with ½ cm/ 0.2in thickness.

Line a large baking tray with baking/parchment paper and place the 2 oval flat bread dough on the tray.

Spread the filling evenly over the 2 flat breads, leaving 2cm/0.8in at the edges as a border with no filling. Fold in the sides to act as a border to keep the filling intact. Squeeze the oval dough at each end to make it pointy.

Beat an egg in a small bowl and mix it with 15ml/1 tablespoon of olive oil. Brush the edges of dough with this mixture. Bake for 25 minutes, until the pides are golden brown and crispy at the edges.

Cut into slices and serve warm.

Afiyet Olsun.

Oval flat breads with minced/ground meat and vegetables
Kıymalı Pide

Serves 6- 8 (makes 2 pides)

Ingredients

For the dough:

300g/10½oz plus 30ml/2 tablespoons all-purpose plain flour

7g/1 sachet of dried yeast

240ml/8fl oz warm water

45ml/3 tablespoons olive oil

Pinch of salt

For the topping:

1 medium onion, finely chopped

400g/14oz minced/ground beef or lamb or mixture

½ green bell pepper or 1 green pointy pepper, finely diced

2 medium tomatoes, de-seeded and diced

15ml/1 tablespoon of lemon juice

15ml/1 tablespoon of olive oil

Salt and freshly ground black pepper to taste

1 beaten egg plus 15ml/1 tablespoon of olive oil to brush the pide

This Kıymalı Pide is our delicious, healthy fast food. Small chunks of meat, spicy Turkish sausage, sucuk or pastırma can also be used here. I like to serve it with the refreshing Shepherd's salad with sumac, Çoban Salata (page 89).

Method

Preheat the oven to 180°C/350°F/Gas Mark 4

Stir in the dried yeast in a small bowl and pour in 120ml/4fl oz warm water. Dissolve the yeast in water. Set aside for the yeast mixture to get frothy for 5 minutes.

Combine the flour and salt in a large bowl. Make a well in the middle and pour in 30ml/2 tablespoons of olive oil and the yeast mixture. Pour in the remaining warm water to the flour mixture. Draw in the flour from the sides and work into a dough. Knead for 3-5 minutes, until you reach a smooth dough. The dough gets sticky as you knead, so pour in the remaining 15ml/1 tablespoon of olive oil and stir in an additional 30ml/2 tablespoons of flour to shape into a soft dough.

Place the dough in large bowl and cover with cling film/plastic wrap. Leave it in a warm place for 1 hour to double in size.

For the topping, heat 15ml/1 tablespoon olive oil in a wide heavy pan and stir in the onions and peppers. Sauté for 2-3 minutes over a medium heat, until they start to soften. Stir in the tomatoes and sauté for another 2 minutes. Pour in the lemon juice and season with salt and ground black pepper. Turn the heat off.

Place the minced/ground meat in a bowl and combine with the cooked vegetables. The topping is ready.

Once the dough has risen, place on a lightly floured surface. Knead the dough for a minute then divide the dough into two pieces and roll into two balls.

On a lightly floured surface, roll the dough balls into 2 oval shapes of 20cm x 40cm/about 8in x 16in, with 0.5cm/0.2in thickness.

Line a large baking tray with baking/parchment paper and place the 2 oval flat bread dough on the tray.

Spread the filling evenly over the 2 flat breads, leaving 2cm/0.8in at the edges as a border with no filling.

Fold in the sides to act as a border to keep the filling intact. Squeeze the dough at each end to make it pointy. Beat an egg in a small bowl and mix it with 1 tablespoon of olive oil. Brush the edges of the dough with this mixture.

Bake for 25-30 minutes, until the pides are golden brown and crispy at the edges.

Cut into slices and serve warm.

Afiyet Olsun.

Chapter Seven

Vegetables

Vegetables

Turkish cuisine, being based on fresh, seasonal produce, offers a fantastic range of vegetarian options. Most of these vegetarian recipes would also be suitable for gluten-free and vegan diets too. We Turks are purists and love the simplicity of cooking our vegetables. We have a special preparation in Turkish cuisine called Zeytinyağlı, meaning "Vegetables cooked in olive oil." With this method of cooking, we simply cook our vegetables with a little water and a generous amount of olive oil. We also often flavour them with herbs and lemon juice. It is healthy and scrumptious. This chapter offers some of the nation's favourite vegetarian dishes, as well as regional specialities like Antakya's Zılk; leafy greens with onions, peppers and pine nuts.

Patlıcan/aubergine/eggplant deserves a special mention as it is Turkey's superstar national vegetable. Prepared in a myriad of ways, there are more than 200 recipes featuring aubergine/eggplant from dips to salads, casseroles, and kebabs. We even make jams out of small, delicate aubergines/eggplants in Antalya region! Drying seasonal vegetables is still common practice especially in southern Turkey – their rich flavours ensuring a constant year-round supply for casseroles in the cooler months. It is a wonderful sight to see long braids of colourful peppers and dark purple aubergines/eggplants hanging to dry outside village homes in the hot summer sun.

Aubergines/eggplants, lentils and peppers cooked in olive oil
Mercimekli Mualla

Serves 4

Ingredients

175g/6oz green lentils, rinsed

2 medium aubergines/eggplants

*2 medium onions,
halved and thinly sliced*

*4 cloves of garlic, crushed and
finely chopped*

*1 red bell pepper, cut in half
and thinly sliced*

*400g/14oz (1 can of) chopped
tomatoes in juice*

60ml/2fl oz olive oil

240ml/8fl oz water

*45ml/3 tablespoons light olive oil
(to sauté aubergines/eggplants)*

5ml/1 teaspoon salt

5ml/1 teaspoon granulated sugar

10ml/2 teaspoons dried mint

*Freshly ground black pepper
to taste*

Crusty bread to serve

Aubergine is the king of vegetables in Turkey. Like a tomato, it is actually classified as a fruit because it has seeds. This scrumptious, traditional recipe, Mercimekli Mualla, is from Antakya and has been cooked in the southern Turkish kitchens for generations. Dried mint and olive oil flavour the green lentils and aubergine/eggplant beautifully. We make this recipe using the Turkish Zeytinyağlı method (vegetables cooked in olive oil) and it's important to let the dish cool in the pan so it can rest and the flavours develop. Passed on to me by my grandmother and mother, I share this recipe with you in the hope you enjoy it as much as we all do.

Method

Put the green lentils in a pan of boiling water, stir and cover. Simmer in low heat for 15 minutes. Drain the water and set aside.

Using a vegetable peeler, peel the aubergine/eggplant in zebra stripes. Then, cut the aubergine/eggplant in half lengthways and cut each half into medium slices. Spread them on a wide tray, sprinkle salt over and leave aside for 15 minutes. Using a paper towel, squeeze the excess water out of the aubergines/eggplants.

Heat the light olive oil in a heavy pan and very lightly sauté the aubergine/eggplant slices for a minute or two. This will help aubergines/eggplants to soften up and start bringing out their lovely sweet flesh.

In a large bowl, combine the partially cooked lentils, onion, garlic, bell peppers, chopped tomatoes, salt, dried mint, olive oil and the sugar. Season with ground black pepper, check the seasoning and add more salt if needed.

In a wide heavy pan, place a layer of the aubergine/eggplant slices. Spread the half of the vegetable mixture over the aubergines/eggplants evenly. Place the remainder of the aubergine/eggplant slices over the top and spread the remaining vegetable mixture over also. Add the water, cover and cook on a medium to low heat for about 35 minutes.

Once cooked, cover and cool the dish in the pan, this will allow the flavours to develop and blend well. Serve at room temperature with some crusty bread.

Afiyet Olsun.

Leafy greens with onions, peppers and pine nuts
Antakya's Zılk inspiration

Serves 4

Ingredients

240g/8oz spring greens (or Swiss chard, kale or spinach), trimmed and finely chopped (including stems)

1 large onion, finely chopped

1 red bell pepper or pointy pepper, finely chopped

½ juice of lemon

30ml/2 tablespoons water

30ml/2 tablespoons olive oil

Salt and ground black pepper to taste

To serve:

60g/2oz pine nuts

10ml/2 teaspoons olive oil

10ml/2 teaspoons red pepper flakes or chili flakes (optional)

This dish is inspired by a vegetable grown in southern Turkey called zılk. It is similar to Swiss chard and locals use either zılk or spinach to make this recipe. Bulgur or lentils are often added to make it a more substantial meal. In this version, I have included sweet, red bell peppers and pine nuts instead of bulgur. Adding a splash of fresh lemon juice and a little heat from red pepper flakes, this delicious dish can be served with any meat or fish main course and pasta.

Method

Heat the olive oil in a wide, heavy pan. Stir in the onions and chopped bell peppers. Sauté over a medium heat for 5 minutes, they will start to soften. Add the chopped spring greens and mix well. Season with salt and ground black pepper. Stir and cook over a medium heat for 3 minutes.

Stir in the lemon juice and 30ml/2 tablespoons water, combine well. Cover and cook for a further 8 minutes under a low to medium heat. The vegetables will still retain a delicious bite to them, turn the heat off.

While the spring greens are cooking, heat 10ml/2 teaspoons olive oil in a small pan.

Stir in the pine nuts and sauté under a low to medium heat for about 3 minutes. Please keep an eye on the pine nuts, as they tend to brown quickly. Turn the heat off.

Combine the pine nuts with the cooked greens, peppers and onions, mix well. Serve hot with red pepper flakes sprinkled over if you like.

Afiyet Olsun.

Green beans cooked in olive oil with vegetables
Zeytinyağlı Taze Fasulye

Serves 4-6

Ingredients

500g/1¼ lb runner(green) beans, trimmed and cut into 3 pieces

1 medium onion, finely chopped

3 cloves garlic, finely chopped

45ml/3 tablespoons olive oil

400g/14oz (1 can of) diced tomatoes

120ml/4fl oz water

10ml/2 teaspoons sugar

Salt and ground black pepper to taste

Lemon wedges to serve

As one of the nation's favourite Zeytinyağlı, Turks traditionally make this recipe with runner beans, but French and dwarf beans work just as well. This is a simple, easy to prepare dish and a delicious way to enjoy green beans. Traditionally, zeytinyağlı dishes (vegetables cooked in olive oil) are prepared in advance and served at room temperature as a meze or vegetable course. Don't forget to include lemon wedges on the side – a light squeeze of lemon juice over the beans adds the perfect finishing touch. Serve this healthy vegetarian dish as an appetizer or with a main course. It can be kept in the fridge for 2-3 days.

Method

Sauté the onion and garlic in olive oil in a wide, heavy pan, for a couple of minutes. Add the green beans and canned tomatoes; stir, combine and cook for another 1 or 2 minutes. Pour over the water, add the sugar, season with salt and ground black pepper. Bring the liquid to the boil, reduce the heat, cover and simmer for about 35 minutes.

Check the seasoning and add more salt if needed. Remove from the heat and set aside to cool in the pan. In Turkish cooking, it is important for the vegetables cooked in olive oil to cool and rest in the pan, for the flavours to blend well.

Transfer to a serving dish and serve with wedges of lemon to squeeze over.

Afiyet Olsun.

Leeks cooked in olive oil with vegetables
Zeytinyağlı Pırasa

Serves 4

Ingredients

500g/1¼ lb leeks, washed, trimmed and sliced into bitesize pieces

1 medium onion, finely chopped

1 medium carrot, cut lengthways and thinly sliced

15ml/1 tablespoon long grain rice, washed and drained

60ml/2fl oz olive oil

240ml/8fl oz hot water

5ml/1 teaspoon sugar

Juice of 1 lemon

Salt and freshly ground black pepper to taste

Lemon wedges to serve

Leeks are native to Anatolia and this method of cooking leeks, (pırasa, as we call it in Turkish) is common in Turkish cuisine. It is traditionally served cold or at room temperature, with wedges of lemon as an appetizer or side dish. Easy to prepare and wholesome, this dish will keep in the fridge for 2 days and is a huge favourite in our home.

Method

In a wide, heavy pan heat the olive oil over a medium heat. Sauté the onions and carrots for 3-4 minutes. Stir in the leeks and the rice, combine well.

Pour in the hot water and lemon juice. Also stir in sugar and season with salt and freshly ground black pepper, give a gentle mix.

Cover and cook gently over low heat for about 25 minutes or until the rice and vegetables are tender. Once cooked, set aside to cool with the lid on. This will help the flavours develop and settle.

Transfer to a serving dish and serve with lemon wedges by the side.

Afiyet Olsun.

Courgette/zucchini fritters with feta and dill
Kabak Mücveri

Serves 4

Ingredients

3 medium courgette/zucchini, grated

200g/7oz Turkish white cheese, beyaz peynir or feta cheese, crumbled

1 medium onion, grated or finely chopped

3 spring onions/scallions, finely chopped

3 garlic cloves, finely chopped

1 small bunch dill, finely chopped

Handful of flat leaf (Italian) parsley, finely chopped

3 eggs, beaten

60ml/4 tablespoons all-purpose/ plain flour

5ml/1 teaspoon Turkish red pepper flakes or chili flakes (optional)

Salt and ground black pepper to taste

Canola oil (or sunflower oil) for shallow frying

For garlic yoghurt:

1 clove of garlic, crushed with salt and finely chopped

240ml/8fl oz plain yoghurt

Courgettes/zucchini, or kabak is a popular summer squash at home and its flower is perfect for stuffing. These fritters, kabak mücveri are a great way to enjoy courgettes/zucchinis. It is important to squeeze out the excess juice from the grated courgettes in this recipe otherwise the fritters will turn out wet and soggy. Serve these light, crispy vegetarian fritters with garlic yoghurt as an appetizer or with a green salad and crusty bread as a light lunch. Smaller bitesize fritters also make an excellent finger food for entertaining.

If you are after a lighter flavour, you can bake the spread, like my mother does, in a greased baking dish at 180°C/350°F/Gas Mark 4 for about 35-40 minutes. Once cool, you can then cut in squares and serve.

Method

Place the grated courgette/zucchini in a colander, sprinkle with a little salt and leave to drain for 15 minutes. Using a tea towel, really squeeze out any excess juice from the courgette/zucchini and put in a large bowl. This is a crucial step as otherwise the moisture would make the fritters soggy.

Transfer the flour to the large bowl and stir in the beaten eggs. Crumble the Turkish white cheese, beyaz peynir or feta cheese and combine in the large bowl. Add the remaining ingredients, season with salt and ground black pepper and combine well into a batter (take care not to add salt if your cheese is already salty).

In a frying pan, heat enough oil to shallow fry. Using a tablespoon, drop the batter mix into the hot oil spoonful by spoonful, leaving space between each one. Fry over a medium heat for about 3 minutes each side until both sides are golden brown. Remove with a straining spoon and drain on an absorbent kitchen paper towel.

For garlic yoghurt, crush a garlic clove with salt and finely chop. Combine the plain yoghurt and garlic and beat until smooth. Add salt to taste.

Serve at room temperature or cold with garlic yoghurt at the side.

Afiyet Olsun.

Baked cauliflower with red onions, feta and dill
Fırında Karnabahar Mücveri

Serves 6

Ingredients

1 medium cauliflower, cut into very small florets

200g/7oz Turkish white cheese or feta cheese, drained and crumbled

60ml/4 tablespoons all-purpose/ plain flour

3 medium eggs, beaten

1 small red onion, finely chopped

3 spring onions/scallions finely chopped

2 garlic cloves, finely chopped

Small bunch of flat leaf (Italian) parsley, finely chopped

Small bunch of fresh dill, finely chopped

30ml/2 tablespoons olive oil

10 ml/2 teaspoons Turkish red pepper flakes or chili flakes

Salt and freshly ground black pepper to taste

22cm x 22cm/7in x 7in baking dish to bake

15ml/1 tablespoon olive oil to grease the baking dish

Wedges of lemon to serve

During one of my culinary tours to Turkey, we had a Turkish cooking class with the lovely Hatice Hanım at Bizimev Hanımeli Restaurant, near the charming Sirince in the Aegean region. We made lightly battered, delicious cauliflower fritters as part of our class. Inspired by this dish, I created this version and tried baking cauliflower with feta, dill and onions in the oven. The result was a great success - baking brought out a sweetness in the cauliflower which balanced nicely with the feta; a lovely dish, packed with flavour.

I serve this baked cauliflower with Cacık yoghurt dip with cucumbers and Shepherd's Salad. It can be served hot or at room temperature with a grilled main course and lemon wedges on the side.

Method

Preheat the oven to 180°C/350°F/Gas Mark 4

Cut the cauliflower into very small florets, wash and drain the excess water in a colander.

Place the cauliflower florets in a large mixing bowl. Stir in the chopped red onions, garlic, spring onions/scallions, parsley, dill, olive oil and the crumbled feta cheese to the bowl. Season with salt, ground black pepper and Turkish red pepper flakes or chili flakes.

With clean hands, mix and combine all the ingredients well. At this stage, you can check the seasoning – add more salt or peppers to your taste. Then stir in the beaten eggs and flour to the cauliflower mixture and combine well.

Grease your baking dish with 15ml/1 tablespoon olive oil and spread the mixture to the baking dish. Bake in the preheated oven at 180°C/350°F/ Gas Mark 4 for 30-35 minutes, until the cauliflower florets have a nice light brown colour on top.

Slice and serve hot or at room temperature with a wedge of lemon at the side.

Afiyet Olsun.

Baked potatoes, peppers and olives with cumin and red pepper flakes
Zeytinli Fırın Patates

Serves 6

Ingredients

1kg/2.2 lb medium potatoes, quartered

2 medium red onions, cut in half and thinly sliced

2 red bell pepper (or pointy pepper), de-seeded, quartered and thinly sliced

12-14 good quality black olives, pitted and halved

15ml/1 tablespoon ground cumin

10ml/2 teaspoons Turkish red pepper flakes or chili flakes

30ml/2 tablespoons olive oil

Salt and ground black pepper to taste

This one-pot vegetarian dish is one of my family's favourites. A touch of warm pungent cumin and spicy red pepper flakes transforms the taste of humble potatoes to a new level of flavour. Use good quality fresh olives as they add a distinctive flavour to the potatoes. Turkish, Italian, Spanish or Greek Kalamata olives will all work well.

Method

Preheat the oven to 200°C/400°F/Gas Mark 6

Put the quartered potatoes in a large enough pan with plenty of cold water. Parboil or partially cook the potatoes for 10 minutes. Drain and set aside.

Heat the olive oil in a pan and stir in the sliced red onions and peppers. Sauté for 3-4 minutes, until they start to soften up, turn the heat off.

Grease the baking tray with a good drizzle (about 30ml/2 tablespoons) of olive oil. Combine the parboiled potatoes, sautéed red onions, peppers and the pitted black olives in the tray. Stir in any remaining olive oil in the pan of the sautéed red onions and peppers to the baking tray.

Sprinkle the ground cumin and red pepper flakes over the vegetables. Season with salt and ground black pepper. Using your hands, combine the spices and the seasoning with the vegetables and olives, giving them a good mix.

Bake for 35 minutes at 200°C/400°F/Gas Mark 6 and serve hot.

Afiyet Olsun.

Chapter Eight

Meat & Poultry

Casseroles, kebabs and regional specialities

Meat & Poultry

Kebabs are synonymous with Turkish cuisine and we Turks love meat, as much as our vegetables. Lamb is our long established meat of choice but beef and poultry have become more popular in recent years as a healthier alternative. With my roots going back to Antakya in southern Turkey, I grew up enjoying succulent homemade kebabs which were often cooked at our local bakery in Long Market, Uzun Çarşı. As children, we would carry my grandmother's tray bake kebab mixture, Tepsi Kebabı to our local bakery in Antakya to bake. I can still remember the glorious aromas of baked kebabs coming from the wood fired oven to this day.

This chapter also features casseroles and regional specialities like my mother's Mevlübi, which is similar to its Middle Eastern cousin Maqluba; layers of succulent meat, aubergines/eggplants and rice cooked together – an impressive dish for entertaining.

Our casseroles and one-pot meals, such as baked Turkish meatballs with vegetables, Fırında Sebzeli Köfte in this section, offer healthy and convenient choices for today's busy lifestyle. Prepared in advance and requiring only a gentle re-heating before serving, the flavours "marry" together for a rich and satisfying meal.

Stuffed courgettes/zucchini with minced/ground meat & chickpeas
Antakya Usulu Kabak Dolması

Serves 4-6

Ingredients

3 chunky courgettes /zucchinis

250g/9oz minced/ground lean beef or lamb

1 onion, finely chopped

3 cloves of garlic, crushed and finely chopped

200g/7oz/½ can of chopped tomatoes

200g/7oz /½ can of cooked chickpeas, rinsed

30ml/2 tablespoons pomegranate molasses, nar ekşisi

30ml/2 tablespoons olive oil

120ml/4fl oz water

15ml/1tablespoon tomato paste

5ml/1teaspoon dried mint

5ml/1 teaspoon Turkish red pepper flakes or chili flakes

Salt and ground black pepper to taste

To serve:

240ml/8fl oz plain yoghurt

1 small garlic clove, crushed with salt and finely chopped

This dish, also known as Sih-el Mahsi, originates from Syria and highlights the Arabic influence on Antakya cuisine; it's an exciting way to enjoy courgettes/zucchinis. Traditionally, the locals in Antakya stuff the courgette as a whole then lightly brown before cooking with the meat sauce. Lentils can be used in the filling too. I prefer my mother's method of cutting the courgette in half lengthways and baking them once they are stuffed. You can prepare this dish ahead of time and the leftovers freeze beautifully. A helpful tip - Save the courgette flesh and use in the bulgur pilaf with courgette recipe, Kabaklı Aş (see page 209).

Method

Preheat the oven to 180°F/350°C/Gas Mark 4

Cut the courgette/zucchini in half and then in lengthways. Using a dessert spoon, carefully scoop out some of the flesh to create a cavity that is large enough to stuff (you can save the flesh of the courgette/zucchini that you scooped out. They are delicious cooked with bulgur, as in Kabaklı Aş).

Mix 1 tablespoon water with the 2 tablespoons pomegranate molasses in a small bowl. Wash the inside of the courgettes/zucchinis with this mixture. Keep the leftover of this delicious juice to be added to the filling mixture.

Heat the oil in a heavy pan. Stir in the onions and garlic and cook until they have a light golden colour. Add the minced/ground meat and sauté for a few minutes. Season with salt and ground black pepper. Stir in the chopped tomatoes, left over pomegranate molasses sauce and the cooked chickpeas, mix well. Add the red pepper flakes and the dried mint, combine well. The filling is ready.

Grease a baking tray and place the courgettes/zucchinis with the scooped side up. Take a spoonful of the filling and stuff the courgette/zucchini halves. Take care not to over fill them. Dilute the tomato paste with the water and pour on the tray. Cover and bake in the oven for about 30 minutes. After this, uncover and bake for a further 10-15 minutes for a lightly browned finish.

In a bowl, mix the plain yoghurt and the garlic. Serve the stuffed courgettes/zucchinis hot, with the garlic yoghurt by the side.

Afiyet Olsun.

Split aubergines/eggplants with minced/ground meat & vegetables
Karnıyarık

Serves 6

Ingredients

3 dark purple medium aubergines/eggplants

340g/12oz minced/ground lean lamb or beef

1 medium onion, finely chopped

4 garlic cloves, finely chopped

400g/14oz (1 can of) chopped tomatoes

30ml/2 tablespoons tomato paste

240ml/8fl oz water

1 small bunch of flat leaf (Italian) parsley, finely chopped

15ml/1 tablespoon olive oil

60ml/2fl oz canola oil for shallow frying

6 thin slices of tomato and green bell peppers, seeded – for decorative topping

5ml/1 teaspoon Turkish red pepper flakes or chili flakes

Salt and freshly ground black pepper

Karnıyarık features the jewel in the crown of Turkish cuisine; the aubergine, otherwise known as the eggplant or patlıcan. This dish is especially close to my heart, as karnıyarık was the first dish I cooked for my husband, Angus, when we were courting. Making karnıyarık involved a lengthy phone call from Scotland (where I was studying) to my mother in Istanbul. As I was getting patlıcan recipe tips from my mother, Angus overheard and asked what the patlıcan was. I explained that it means aubergine/eggplant. Then he said: "it sounds rather nice, I think I will call you patlıcan!" My name between us from then on became patlıcan, and sometimes just patlı and I am rather fond of it.

You can cook karnıyarık ahead of time and gently reheat in the oven. It also freezes well, once cooked. This recipe is adapted from Angie Mitchell's Turkish cookery book, Secrets of the Turkish Kitchen.

Method

Preheat oven to 180°C/350°F/Gas Mark 4

Cut the aubergines/eggplants in half lengthways leaving the stalk intact. In each half of the aubergine, cut a deep split lengthways without cutting through to the skin on the opposite side and leaving ½in/13mm uncut at either end. Sprinkle salt over the flesh side of the aubergines and leave them aside for 15 minutes.

Pour in the olive oil into a heavy pan and sauté the onions until soft. Add the minced/ground lamb (or beef) and cook until all the moisture is absorbed. Stir in the garlic, chopped tomatoes, tomato paste and red pepper flakes. Season with salt and freshly ground black pepper, mix well. Continue cooking for a further couple of minutes. Turn the heat off and stir in most of the chopped parsley. Seasoning is important, so please check the seasoning of the mixture and add more salt or pepper if you would like.

Dry the aubergines/eggplants with kitchen towel thoroughly. Pour in the canola oil on a wide, heavy pan and lightly brown the aubergines/eggplants evenly on both sides. Then place the aubergine/eggplant halves into a baking dish with the split sides facing up. Spoon the filling into the cavity of the aubergine/eggplant halves. On the top of each filled aubergine/eggplant, put a slice of tomato and a green bell pepper. Mix the water with a drizzle of olive oil. Pour this mixture on the baking tray. Cover and bake in the pre-heated oven for about 40 minutes. Remove the cover and continue baking for another 10 minutes or until they are tender and the aubergines/eggplants are nicely browned on top.

Serve hot with plain rice and a dollop of plain yoghurt by the side.

Afiyet Olsun.

Baked Turkish meatballs with vegetables
Fırında Sebzeli Köfte

Serves 4-6

Ingredients

For the köfte (meatballs)

450g/1lb minced/ground lamb, beef or mixture

1 medium onion, grated

2 slices of stale bread, soaked in water and squeezed dry

1 egg, beaten

1 bunch of finely chopped flat leaf (Italian) parsley

5ml/1 teaspoon ground cumin

5ml/1 teaspoon Turkish red pepper flakes or chili flakes

5ml/1 teaspoon salt

Freshly ground black pepper to taste

Small bowl of water for kneading kofte and for getting your hands wet

And the rest:

450g/1lb medium potatoes, sliced as thin apple quadrants

1 green, red or yellow bell pepper, de-seeded and sliced

1 medium carrot, coarsely sliced

1 aubergine/eggplant, cut in half lengthways and sliced

4 garlic cloves, finely chopped

400g/14oz (1 can of) chopped tomatoes

15 ml/1 tablespoon tomato paste

30ml/2 tablespoons olive oil

240ml/8fl oz water

Salt and freshly ground black pepper to taste

5ml/1 teaspoon Turkish red pepper flakes or chili flakes

Esnaf Lokantası is a simple, no-frills, traditional style restaurant in Turkey serving homemade slow cooked casseroles. Dishes are set up buffet style and you help yourself to a hot dinner at a very reasonable price – and best of all usually you don't have to wait!

This meatball and vegetable casserole is typical lokanta food and easy to make at home. Cooked on the stove top or baked in the oven, this casserole can also be made in advance. It makes a complete and hearty weekday dinner served with plain rice or bulgur pilaf. I like to add seasonal vegetables to this meatball casserole – courgettes/zucchinis, runner beans and peas all work well. I usually double this casserole recipe and freeze half the portion.

Method

Preheat oven to 180°C/350°F/Gas Mark 4

Discard the crusts of the bread, soak in the water and squeeze dry. Then crumble them into a large bowl. Add all the köfte, meatballs ingredients except the meat and knead well. This will soften the onions and enable the spices to blend in the mixture evenly. Add the minced meat/ground meat and knead well again until the mixture resembles a soft dough. With wet hands take a piece the size of a large walnut and roll into a large finger shape about 1 inch thick. Continue until all the mixture is used. The meatballs can now be covered and stored in the fridge until required.

Using a vegetable peeler, peel the aubergine/eggplant lengthways in stripes like the pattern on a zebra. Slice the aubergine/eggplant lengthways, about 12.5mm/½in thick. Then cut each slice into three to four chunky parts. Sprinkle some salt over them and leave for about 15 minutes. Squeeze out their moisture with a paper towel.

In an oven dish, spread the vegetables. Coat the vegetables with the olive oil, tomato paste, red pepper flakes, salt and pepper. Using your hands, mix the vegetables and make sure they all get this lovely coating. Place the meatballs between the vegetables. Add the chopped tomatoes and water, gently mix well. Bake in the oven for about 40-45 minutes or until the potatoes are soft and the sauce has thickened.

Afiyet Olsun.

Upside down rice with layers of aubergine/eggplant, chicken and potatoes | *Mevlübi*

Serves 4

Ingredients

500g/1¼lb boneless chicken thighs or breasts, cut in chunks

3 medium potatoes, peeled and sliced as half-moon shape

2 small aubergines/eggplants, cut lengthways and sliced crossways

1 small onion, cut in half and thinly sliced

350g/12oz long grain rice

900ml/1½ pints hot water

15ml/1 tablespoon of salted butter

Sunflower or canola oil for shallow frying

Salt and ground black pepper to taste

Bowl of warm salted water to wash the rice

For marinating the chicken:

15ml/1 tablespoon plain yoghurt

30ml/2 tablespoons olive oil

5ml/1 teaspoon cumin

5ml/1 teaspoon oregano

10ml/2 teaspoons tomato paste

5ml/1 teaspoon red pepper flakes

Salt and ground black pepper to taste

Non-stick deep pan to cook Mevlübi

Mevlübi, also known as Maklube, is a very special dish for us. This glorious upside-down rice with layers of meat and vegetables appears on my mother's table at every special occasion. Mevlübi has many versions throughout the Middle East and this recipe is from my grandmother in Antakya. Lamb and beef can be used instead of chicken here. It is best to cook Mevlübi at least 20 minutes before serving so it can "rest" and the flavours have more depth. Mevlübi makes an impressive main course for entertaining guests, or a healthy, all-in-one family weeknight dinner.

Method

In a large bowl, combine the marinate ingredients and the chicken pieces well. You can prepare this marinade a day ahead of time and keep in the fridge covered, until cooking time.

Cut the aubergines/eggplants lengthways and slice in half-moon or circle shape (if small enough), about 2cm/0.8in thick. Lay the aubergines/eggplants on a tray and sprinkle salt over and let the moisture come out for 15 minutes. Then squeeze out any further moisture from the aubergines/eggplants using a paper towel.

Pour about 30ml/2 tablespoons of sunflower or canola oil on a non-stick, deep pan you will be cooking Mevlübi. Sauté the aubergine/eggplant slices for a few minutes at each side. Place the paper towel on a wide tray and transfer the aubergines/eggplants to the tray to drain excess oil. Sauté the potatoes, onions and the chicken pieces (all separately) for 3-4 minutes in the pan and place on the tray next to the aubergines/eggplants.

Layer the sautéed chicken pieces to cover the whole surface at the bottom of the same non-stick deep pan. Then layer the aubergine/eggplant slices over the chicken evenly, followed by the potato slices and the onions.

Soak the rice in warm salted water for 15 minutes, then drain this water and rinse the rice with cold water. Spread the rice over the potato and onion layer evenly. Pour the hot water over, season with salt and ground black pepper and cover. Start cooking on the medium heat until it starts bubbling. Then turn the heat to low, cover and continue cooking until the rice is cooked and the water has been absorbed for about 20-25 minutes. Once the liquid is absorbed, place a tablespoon of butter in the middle of the rice and push down towards the middle. Add two tablespoons of hot water over the rice, cover and cook for another 10 minutes on a very low heat. Once the rice is fully cooked, turn the heat off, put a paper towel over and cover with the lid tightly. Make sure you cook Mevlübi about 20 minutes before you serve. That will give the dish a chance to rest and all the flavours to blend together.

Once it is rested, turn the Mevlübi pan over a big serving plate (larger than the pan) or tray gently. Slowly and gently, lift the pan and, as if by magic, the dish should come out like a cake.

Afiyet Olsun.

Bulgur balls with aubergine/eggplant, tomato, dried mint sauce
Patlıcanlı Ekşi Aşı

Serves 4

Ingredients

2 medium aubergines/eggplants

1 medium onion, finely chopped

3 garlic cloves, finely chopped

2 cans of 400g/14oz good quality plum tomatoes

10ml/2 teaspoons red pepper paste

15ml/1 tablespoon tomato paste

15ml/1 tablespoon pomegranate molasses

45ml/3 tablespoons olive oil

750ml/1.3 pints water

10ml/2 teaspoons dried mint

5ml/1 teaspoon Turkish red pepper flakes or chili flakes

Salt and ground black pepper to taste

For the bulgur dough:

110g/4oz fine bulgur, köftelik bulgur (if you can only get coarse bulgur, you can pulse it a few times in a food processor to make it fine)

90ml/3fl oz warm water to wet the bulgur and 120ml/4fl oz warm water to knead the bulgur

40g/1½oz coarse semolina

30ml/2 tablespoons warm water for semolina

60g/2oz extra lean (double grind) minced/ground beef

15ml/1 tablespoon Turkish hot pepper paste, biber salçası

5ml/1 teaspoon ground cumin

5ml/1 teaspoons Turkish red pepper flakes or chili flakes

Salt to taste

Bowl of cold water for shaping the bulgar balls

This is a speciality from Antakya, made when ripe tomatoes are in season. If ripe tomatoes aren't available, good quality tinned tomatoes will work just as well. Dried mint adds a fresh flavour and the pomegranate molasses complete the finishing touch. The meaty-like aubergines/eggplants melt in the mouth in this dish and complement the bulgur balls well. Omit the minced/ground beef for a vegetarian version.

Method

First make the bulgur balls. Place the fine bulgur in a large mixing bowl. Stir in the red pepper paste, cumin, salt and red pepper flakes and mix them all well. Then pour the 90ml/3fl oz warm water all over it. Using your hands, give the mixture a good mix and let it absorb the water for 10 minutes. In the meantime, place the semolina in a separate bowl and stir in the 30ml/2 tablespoons warm water. Knead and turn the semolina mixture into a soft dough. Semolina is important here as it helps to bind the bulgur dough.

Have the 120ml/4fl oz warm water bowl next to you and start kneading the bulgur mixture for about 5 minutes. Wet your hands continuously while kneading. Stir in the semolina dough and knead together for another 5 minutes. Add the meat and knead for 10 minutes, until you get a smooth dough.

Have a bowl of cold water aside to shape the small round bulgur balls. Wet your hands and take a large cherry size bulgur dough into your palm and shape it like a small ball. Place the bulgur balls side-by-side on a tray and continue until you finish all the bulgur dough.

Quarter the aubergines then slice each piece diagonally in 3cm/about 1in chunks. Lay them on a tray and season with salt. Leave for about 15 minutes. Drain the excess moisture by squeezing them with a paper towel.

Place the plum tomatoes into a food processor and process until you achieve a coarse purée.

In a deep, heavy pan, pour in the olive oil and stir in the aubergines/eggplants. Sauté for 3-4 minutes, until they have a nice golden colour. Place the sautéed aubergines/eggplants on a wide plate over a paper towel to get rid of the excess oil. Stir in the garlic and the onions and sauté for another 2-3 minutes.

Pour in the puréed tomato, tomato paste, red pepper paste and the water to the pan. Stir in the aubergines/eggplants, season with salt and freshly ground pepper. Combine well gently. Cover and cook on a medium heat for 15 minutes.

Then carefully drop the bulgur balls into the pan and combine well. Cover and cook on a low heat for another 25 minutes.

Stir in the pomegranate molasses, dried mint and red pepper flakes, combine well. Turn the heat off and serve warm with pide bread or crusty bread aside.

Afiyet Olsun.

Dried aubergines/eggplants and peppers, stuffed with minced/ground meat & aromatic rice | *Kuru Patlıcan ve Biber Dolması*

Serves 6-8

Ingredients

12 dried aubergine/eggplant shells and 15 dried small bell pepper shells, string removed

1 large onion, grated or finely chopped

200g/7oz long grain rice, rinsed

400g/14oz minced/ground beef

3 garlic cloves, finely chopped

Handful of flat leaf (Italian) parsley, finely chopped

15ml/1 tablespoon Turkish red pepper paste, biber salçası – optional

15ml/1 tablespoon tomato paste

30ml/2 tablespoons pomegranate molasses, nar ekşisi

15ml/1 tablespoon olive oil (for the filling)

5ml/1 teaspoon ground cumin

10ml/2 teaspoons dried mint

Salt and freshly ground black pepper to taste

2 tomatoes, coarsely chopped, as a cap (optional)

30ml/ 2 tablespoons olive oil (for cooking)

360ml/12fl oz water for cooking

Garlicky yoghurt to serve

Turkish red pepper flakes or chili flakes to serve

Dried aubergines/eggplants and peppers are a real southern Turkish treat and they are always a popular talking point at my Turkish cookery classes. When aubergines and bell peppers are in season, some of the harvest in southern Turkey is dried out for use in the winter months. The flesh is scooped out and the shells are tied together with string to dry out in the hot summer sun creating a rich concentration of flavour packed in each dried out shell. I add a generous pinch of fragrant dried mint, tangy pomegranate molasses and red pepper paste to the stuffing mixture, as we do in southern Turkey. Bulgur can be used instead of rice and, of course, omit the meat if you wish to make this a vegetarian dish.

Method

Cut the strings of the dried aubergines/eggplants and peppers and place in a large pan of boiling water. Blanch them for 3 minutes to rehydrate. Afterwards, gently place them on another pan with cold water for 2 minutes, to give them a "cold bath"; this will help them to retain their colour and texture and not to break apart. Then gently place the hydrated dried peppers and aubergines/eggplants in a colander, ready to be stuffed.

Place the onions, garlic, red pepper paste (if using), tomato paste, parsley, 1 tablespoon of olive oil and spices in a large bowl. Season with salt and ground black pepper to your taste. Knead this mixture with your hands for a minute, making sure all are blended well (this stage also helps to soften the onions). Stir in the minced/ground meat, rice and pomegranate molasses to the bowl and mix well. The filling is now ready.

Get a wide, heavy pan and pour in the 30ml/2 tablespoons of olive oil. Spoon the filling mixture carefully into each pepper and aubergine/eggplant, pressing gently for the filling to settle in. Make sure to leave about 1cm/0.4in space at top for the filling to cook and expand. You can seal the tops with a piece of tomato as a cap or you may press the edges together for a gentle close. Place them upright, side-by-side, packed tightly (it would be ideal to place the stuffed peppers and aubergines/eggplants side-by-side in one layer if you can).

Pour the water over and around the stuffed peppers and aubergines/eggplants. The water should cover half of the length of the stuffed vegetables. Bring the liquid to the boil then reduce the heat, cover and cook gently for 30-35 minutes or until the filling is cooked.

Serve hot with Turkish red pepper flakes or chili flakes sprinkled over them, if you like. Thick plain yoghurt mixed with a little crushed garlic goes very well with these stuffed eggplants and peppers.

Afiyet Olsun.

Stuffed peppers and courgettes/zucchinis with bulgur and pomegranate molasses | *Bulgurlu Dolma*

Serves 6-8

Ingredients

3 medium sized courgettes/zucchinis

3 medium size bell peppers

30ml/2 tablespoons pomegranate molasses mixed with 15ml/1 tablespoon of water

3 small tomatoes, cut coarsely (to cap the dolmas)

4 cloves of garlic, crushed and cut in half

For the filling:

110g/4oz minced/ground beef or lamb

115g/4oz coarse bulgur wheat

1 medium onion, finely chopped or grated

Handful of flat leaf (Italian) parsley, finely chopped

15ml/1 tablespoon olive oil

15ml/1 tablespoon concentrated tomato paste or red pepper paste

5ml/1 teaspoon of Turkish red pepper flakes or chili flakes

5ml/1 teaspoon ground cumin

5ml/1 teaspoon dried mint

Salt and ground black pepper to taste

Small bowl of plain yoghurt to serve

This bulgurlu dolma is a much loved family recipe and popular with my blog readers. Bulgur grain features heavily in Antakya cuisine and makes a perfect companion with the region's pomegranate molasses and red pepper paste, biber salçası. I love bulgur's nutty wholesome flavour. The typical Antakya preparation removes the vegetable's seeds and flesh, then washes the shell with pomegranate molasses and some water. The tangy, sweet molasses are absorbed into the vegetable for a unique, rich flavour. Use tomato paste instead of red pepper paste if you prefer a milder flavour in the filling. I hope you enjoy this delicious dolma with its robust flavours.

Method

Place the minced/ground meat in a large bowl and stir in the rest of the filling ingredients. Season and knead, until all blended well. The filling is ready.

Now, let's prepare the vegetables. Cut the stalk ends of the peppers and save them aside (we will need them to cap the stuffed peppers later). Scoop out the seeds of the peppers.

Cut the courgettes/zucchinis in half. Scoop out the flesh of the courgettes/ zucchinis with the help of a long coffee spoon (in Antakya, we use a long and thin scooping device made just for that purpose). Carefully remove some of the flesh to create a cavity that is large enough to stuff. Take care to leave the bottom of the courgettes/zucchinis intact (I Iike to save the flesh of the courgettes/zucchinis, as they go very well in the Bulgur pilaf with tomato and courgette/zucchini, Kabaklı Aş recipe at page 209).

Mix the water with the pomegranate molasses and wash the inside of the peppers and courgettes/zucchinis with this mixture. Add the left overs of this delicious juice to the filling mixture, combine well.

Take a couple of spoonfuls of the filling mixture and pack it into the vegetables. Take care not to overfill to the top, as bulgur will need a little space to expand. Place the stalk ends to the peppers and the chopped tomatoes for the courgettes/zucchinis as lids. Place the stuffed vegetables upright, packed tightly, in a heavy pan. Pour a couple of cups of water into the pan, until it covers half of the vegetables. Stir in the cloves of garlic and cover. Bring the liquid to the boil, then reduce the heat and cook gently for about 40 minutes or until the vegetables are tender.

Serve hot with plain natural yoghurt.

Afiyet Olsun.

Stuffed cabbage rolls with bulgur & minced/ground meat
Bulgurlu Lahana Sarması

Serves 6
Ingredients

200g/7oz coarse bulgur

1 large cabbage (which yields about 20 large to medium cabbage leaves)

1 medium onion, finely chopped

225g/8oz minced/ground beef or lamb

Small bunch of parsley leaves, finely chopped

30ml/2 tablespoons olive oil

15ml/1 tablespoon dried mint

5ml/1 teaspoon ground cumin

5ml/1 teaspoon Turkish red pepper flakes or chili flakes

Salt and freshly ground black pepper to taste

For the sauce:

4 cloves of garlic, crushed with salt and finely chopped

15ml/1 tablespoon olive oil

Juice of 1 lemon

570ml/1 pint water

15ml/1 tablespoon tomato paste

Dried mint and red pepper flakes to decorate

Plain yoghurt to serve

We Turks love stuffed vegetables and this stuffed cabbage leaves recipe, Antakya style, is one my family ranks very highly.

Dolma is the term used for stuffed vegetables and sarma is the term used for stuffed vine leaves or cabbage leaves in Turkish. My mother made these lahana sarma often when I was a child. I was always the happy "quality check" – eager for a sample when the rolls were cooked.

Method

Bring a large saucepan of salted water to the boil. Trim the bottom root and place the cabbage as a whole in the pan with boiling water and simmer for 8 minutes.

Remove the cabbage and leave it to cool. Then take a sharp knife and cut the outer leaves from the main stalk. The rest of the leaves will start to peel off one-by-one without breaking. Peel off about 20 large to medium leaves for rolling and set them aside (please save the hard stalk or the hard middle part of the cabbage leaves; they are delicious in Bulgurlu Lahana Kapuska recipe at page 217).

For the filling; combine the bulgur, chopped onion, parsley, olive oil, dried mint, cumin, red pepper flakes, salt and freshly ground black pepper in a large bowl. Knead well with your hands for a few minutes. Stir in the minced/ground meat and knead for another minute to combine well.

With a sharp knife, carefully trim and make a V shape cut to remove the thickest part of the stalk from the base of each cabbage leaf. Place 1 to 1½ tablespoon of the filling (depending on the size of the leaf) in the middle of the leaf. Fold in the sides and then roll the leaf up tightly. Repeat with the remaining leaves and filling.

Place the rolled leaves tightly in a heavy pan with seam side down, do the second layer too and pack tightly.

For the sauce, mix together the water, olive oil, lemon juice, tomato paste and chopped garlic in a bowl. Season with salt and freshly ground black pepper to your taste. Pour this sauce over the rolled cabbage leaves (the water should just about cover the top of the rolled cabbage leaves). Place a plate on top of the leaves to stop them unravelling during cooking.

Cover the pan and cook on a low heat over a stove top or burner for 40-45 minutes, simmering gently. Once the cabbage rolls are cooked, serve hot, decorated with dried mint and red pepper flakes. Plain yoghurt complements these delicious cabbage rolls with bulgur filling, bulgurlu lahana sarması, beautifully.

Afiyet Olsun.

Antakya's tray bake kebab with vegetables
Tepsi Kebabı

Serves 6-8

Ingredients

For the meat mixture:

1kg/2¼ lb minced/ground beef or lamb (or combination)

2 medium onions, finely chopped

4 cloves of garlic, crushed and finely chopped

½ red pointy (or bell) pepper, finely chopped

1 bunch of flat leaf (Italian) parsley, finely chopped

10ml/2 teaspoons red pepper flakes

5ml/1 teaspoon ground cumin

Salt and ground black pepper to taste

For the rest:

1 medium potato, quartered and thinly sliced

1 tomato, cut into wedges

½ red pointy (or bell) pepper, sliced lengthways

½ green pointy (or bell) pepper, sliced lengthways

For the tomato sauce:

15ml/1 tablespoon tomato paste

240ml/8fl oz water

15ml/1 tablespoon olive oil

Salt and ground black pepper to taste

Having spent many happy childhood holidays at our hometown Antakya (ancient Antioch), I used to love watching the two most inspirational women in my life. My grandma and mum. They used to prepare this kebab mixture on a great big round baking tray. Then with older cousins, we grandchildren would toddle off to Antakya's ancient winding roads, to take the kebab mixture to our local bakery in Long Market, Uzun Çarşı, for this feast to be baked. We would be back in an hour or so to pick up this delicious kebab, whose smells would fill the whole bakery, delicious memories.

Potato slices aren't traditionally, on the kebab. But my mother cleverly divides the kebab into wedges and cooks the potatoes alongside, which helps the meat to cook evenly in less time and the potatoes soak up the delicious kebab juices. So I am sharing my mother's version of Tepsi Kebabı here.

Method

Preheat the oven to 180°C/350°F/Gas Mark 4

In a large bowl, mix the onion, garlic, red peppers, parsley, cumin and red pepper flakes. Season with salt and ground black pepper and knead well with your hands for a few minutes, until all the ingredients combined and spices blended in. Stir in the minced/ground meat to the mixture and again with using your hands, knead well until all combined thoroughly.

Grease a round baking tray with a little olive oil and spread the meat mixture onto the tray. Using your hands, press the meat and spread evenly and thinly (height about ½cm/0.20in), retaining the round shape. Make sure the spread goes around the edges; once cooked, the meat will shrink an inch or two.

Slice the meat spread into wedges. Place the sliced potatoes along these edges. Spread the slices of red and green pointy (or bell) peppers and tomatoes over the top of each wedge of the meat mixture. Season well with salt and ground black pepper.

Mix the tomato paste, water and olive oil in a small bowl, season with salt and ground pepper. Pour this mixture over the vegetables and kebab. Bake in the pre-heated oven for about 40-45 minutes until the meat and vegetables have cooked well.

Serve with plain rice and some plain yoghurt, if you like.

Afiyet Olsun.

Antakya's Arab kebab with aubergines/eggplants
Patlıcanlı Arap Kebabı

Serves 4-6

Ingredients

500g/1¼ lb minced/ground beef or lamb

3 medium onions, finely chopped

3 garlic cloves, finely chopped

1 medium size aubergine/eggplant, finely diced

1 green bell (or pointy) pepper, finely chopped

400g/14oz can of good quality chopped tomatoes

15ml/1 tablespoon red pepper paste (or tomato paste, if you prefer a milder taste)

30ml/2 tablespoons olive oil

360ml/12fl oz hot water

1 bunch of flat leaf (Italian) parsley, finely chopped

5-10ml/1-2 teaspoons Turkish red pepper flakes or chili flakes

Salt and freshly ground black pepper to taste

3 medium potatoes, skinned and halved (to be used for the potato and bulgur patties, if you like)

Arap Kebabı finds its origins from the arab community living in Antakya and has been greatly enjoyed in the region. Antakya is a city rich in history and has a happy acceptance of a range of traditions, with people from many religions and ethnic backgrounds who have lived side-by-side for centuries.

I like the simplicity of this recipe and the natural sweetness of onions really enhances the dish's flavours. While aubergines/eggplants are not used in traditional Arap Kebabı, I've tweaked the recipe because the aubergine's/eggplant's sweet, meaty-like texture goes so well in this dish. Red pepper paste, biber salçası, is often used with these kebabs for a richer, spicier flavor. Note: If you prefer a milder taste, substitute with 1 tablespoon of tomato paste.

Potato and bulgur patties go very well with this dish. I cook 2-3 potatoes with Arap Kebabı to soak up the wonderful juices and then use the cooked potatoes to make the patties (see page 221, for the recipe). Dipping these patties in the Arap Kebabı sauce is just heavenly.

Method

Cut each aubergine/eggplant length wise and then into about 2cm/nearly about 1in cubes, lay them on a wide flat tray and season with salt. This will help the moisture to come out of the aubergines/eggplants. Leave for about 15 minutes. Drain the excess moisture from the aubergines/eggplants by squeezing them with a paper towel.

Heat the oil in a large wide pan and sauté the onions for a couple of minutes until they start to soften. Stir in the minced/ground meat and sauté for another couple of minutes. Add the aubergine/eggplant, garlic, green pepper and cook for further 4-5 minutes. Stir in the chopped tomatoes, red pepper paste (or tomato paste if preferred) and the hot water, giving a good mix. Add the potatoes to the mixture. Season with salt, ground black pepper and red pepper flakes, combine well.

Cover the pan and gently simmer for about 30 minutes on a low to medium heat, until all the ingredients have cooked and the sauce thickened. Stir in the chopped parsley and combine well, the Arap Kebabı is ready. The end result should have a good amount of juice/liquid, as we would like to dip the potato and bulgur patties into this sauce. Take the cooked potatoes out to be used in the potato and bulgur patties if you like.

Afiyet Olsun.

Lamb kebabs with pistachios and roasted vegetables
Fıstıklı Kebap

Serves 4

Ingredients

For the kebabs:

500g/1¼ lb minced/ground lamb (or beef or a mixture)

1 medium onion, grated or very finely chopped

4 garlic cloves, crushed and finely chopped

60ml/4 tablespoons of pistachios, shelled

1 bunch of flat leaf (Italian) parsley, finely chopped

5ml/1 teaspoon Turkish red pepper flakes or chili flakes

5ml/1 teaspoon freshly ground black pepper

Salt to taste

A small bowl of water with a drizzle of olive oil to help shape the kebabs

For the roasted vegetables:

3 colourful bell peppers, deseeded and cut in thick slices lengthways OR

10 sweet and chilli small, colorful peppers, cut in half lengthways and de-seeded

4 medium tomatoes, halved and cut into chunky slices

1 medium onion, halved and cut into chunky slices

45ml/3 tablespoons olive oil

Salt and freshly ground black pepper to taste

1 large flat bread or 4 pita bread, sliced lengthways

Plain yoghurt to serve

Cooking pistachios with kebabs is a southern Turkish speciality and the rich, nutty flavour is outstanding. The Gaziantep region in Turkey grows some of the finest quality pistachios, referred as the "edible emeralds". These kebabs are truly amazing when chargrilled on the barbecue in summer, but are also equally delicious grilled in the oven. With flat breads as the base and roasted vegetables by the side, this succulent kebab is the real deal when entertaining.

Method

Preheat the oven to 200°C/400°F/Gas Mark 6

First roast your vegetables. Place the onion, peppers and tomatoes on a baking tray. Drizzle the olive oil over, season with salt and ground black pepper. Give them all a good mix to make sure all the vegetables are coated with olive oil and the seasoning. Bake in the oven for 35–40 minutes, giving them a mix half way. I like to roast the vegetables rather than grilling, to save and enjoy all the wonderful juices of them over the flat bread.

While the vegetables are roasting, prepare the kebabs. First have a small bowl of water, drizzled with olive oil ready aside, to knead and help shape the kebabs into the skewers. Pulse the shelled pistachios in a food processor a few times, until it is grainy but still have a bite to them. Place the minced/ground meat in a large bowl. Stir in the pistachios, chopped onions, garlic and parsley. Season with salt and ground black pepper, add the red pepper or chili flakes. Wet your hands in the water and olive oil mixture and knead well to a smooth mixture. Cover and rest the mixture in the fridge for about 10-15 minutes or until the vegetables are roasted in the oven.

Once the vegetables are chargrilled, take the tray out of the oven, cover and set aside. Put the grill onto its highest setting and start shaping the kebabs. Take a handful of the meat mixture and press it around the grilling skewer into a shape of a flat sausage. Wet your hands with the water and olive oil mixture; this will keep the meat moist and intact.

Cook the kebabs under the grill/broiler for about 4 minutes or until they are golden and cooked through that side. Then place the sliced flat bread or pita bread on a tray and put the tray under the grill, at the bottom of the kebabs. Turn the kebabs and cook for a further 3-4 minutes or until they are golden on the other side also.

Also, at this stage place the roasted vegetables back to the oven to keep them warm.

Once the kebabs are cooked, prepare your serving tray. Put the grilled, warm flat bread slices side-by-side on the tray. Place the kebab skewers in the middle and the roasted vegetables at each side. Serve with a dollop of plain yoghurt by the side.

Afiyet Olsun.

Baked aubergine/eggplant kebab with yoghurt and spices marinated chicken | *Patlıcanlı Kebap*

Serves 4-6

Ingredients

2 medium aubergines/eggplants

700g/1½ lb boneless chicken thighs or chicken breast, skinned and cut into 4x4cm/1.6in x 1.6in chunks

2 red pointy or bell peppers, de-seeded and sliced into chunks

1 green pointy or bell pepper, de-seeded and sliced into chunks

1 medium onion, coarsely chopped

45ml/3 tablespoons of olive oil

Salt and ground black pepper to taste

For the chicken marinade:

2 garlic cloves, finely chopped

30ml/2 tablespoons plain whole milk yoghurt

15ml/1 tablespoon tomato paste

10ml/2 teaspoons Turkish red pepper paste (optional)

5ml/1 teaspoon Turkish red pepper flakes or chili flakes

Salt and ground black pepper to taste

30ml/2 tablespoons of olive oil to sauté the marinated chicken

For the sauce:

5-10ml/1-2 teaspoons red pepper flakes

15ml/1 tablespoon tomato paste

360ml/12fl oz water

This is a typical southern Turkish style kebab that can be prepared at home. The aubergines/eggplants are double baked in this recipe, which intensifies their flavour. In Gaziantep and Antakya, locals use the leftover barbecued aubergines/eggplants to make this delicious kebab the next day. I hope you enjoy recreating this impressive dish.

Tip: Marinating the chicken in yoghurt, olive oil, red pepper paste, biber salçası and spices is really well worth the effort; it tenderizes the chicken and enables the flavours to blend well.

Method

Preheat the oven to 180°C/350°F/Gas Mark 4

Peel the aubergines/eggplants into zebra-like stripes, using a vegetable peeler or a small knife. Cut the aubergines/eggplants lengthways then into 1cm/0.4in thick slices. Place the slices on a tray and sprinkle salt over them (the salt will help extract the bitter juices out of the aubergines/eggplants). Set aside for 15 minutes.

Prepare the marinade for the chicken. Place the chicken pieces in a large bowl. Stir in the yoghurt, garlic, tomato paste, red pepper paste (if using) and red pepper flakes. Season with salt and ground black pepper to your taste. Combine and mix the chicken pieces with the marinade. Cover the marinade and leave in the fridge for 30 minutes (you can prepare this marinade ahead of time, even overnight and leave in the fridge).

Using kitchen paper towel, squeeze the excess moisture out of the aubergines/eggplants. Place the aubergines/eggplants on a tray and drizzle 3 tablespoons of olive oil over them. Coat the pieces with the olive oil and partially bake in the preheated oven for 20 minutes.

Heat the olive oil in a large heavy pan and stir in the marinated chicken pieces. Sauté over a medium to high heat for 4-5 minutes, then turn the heat off.

Once the aubergine/eggplant slices are partially baked, prepare the chicken and aubergine/eggplant and bake with vegetables. In a large baking dish, place a chicken piece next to the onion, pepper (alternating red and green pepper pieces) and aubergine/eggplant slices. Keep on placing chicken and vegetables in this order side-by-side, until all the chicken and vegetables are layered. Spread any remaining aubergine/eggplant slices at the top.

To prepare the sauce, stir in the tomato paste, red pepper flakes and the water to the pan used for sautéing the chicken. Combine all, also using any leftover chicken marinade sauce in the pan. Pour in this mixture over your tray with the chicken, aubergine/eggplant and vegetables.

Bake in the preheated oven for 35-40 minutes, until chicken and vegetables are cooked and have turned a light golden colour.

Serve hot with plain rice or bulgur pilaf at the side.

Afiyet Olsun.

203

Chapter Nine

Bulgur, Rice & Legumes

Bulgur, Rice & Legumes

Bulgur wheat, rice and legumes are an important part of the Turkish diet and I am a huge fan of bulgur. Bulgur wheat is a grain made from cooked wheat berries, which have the bran removed and are then dried and pounded. It is high in fibre, low in fat and rich in protein and minerals and I adore its nutty texture. Bulgur wheat is a major ingredient especially in southern Turkish cuisine. There are two main varieties, fine and coarse bulgur. Meals made with coarse bulgur are called Aş in southern Turkish cuisine and can be a hearty and nourishing meal on their own.

Bulgur can also be cooked with lentils, the ancient grain freekeh, and meat or vegetables.

İnce bulgur is a finer ground and is used in salads such as in Kısır, in patties like in bulgur and potato patties or in Oruk, the Turkish version of baked kibbeh, with minced meat and walnut filling.

Pilaf (or Pilav, as we call it in my native tongue) is a Turkish style rice course - a much loved accompaniment to meat-based courses and stews. İç Pilav, Pilaf with lamb liver, pine nuts and currants, can also be a meal in itself. Lentils, chickpeas and beans can also be cooked with vegetables or with bulgur or rice, for a wholesome, substantial meal.

Bulgur pilaf with courgette/zucchini, onions & tomatoes
Kabaklı Aş

Serves 4-6

Ingredients

2 medium courgettes/zucchini, quartered and thinly sliced

1 onion, finely chopped

350g/12oz bulgur wheat, rinsed and drained

400g/14oz (1 can of) chopped tomatoes

750ml/1.3 pints hot water

30ml/2 tablespoons olive oil

5ml/1 teaspoon dried mint

5ml/1 teaspoon red pepper flakes

Salt and ground black pepper to taste

This wholesome dish is from southern Turkey and is particularly enjoyed in the Antakya region. Bulgur cooked this way with vegetables is called Aş in Antakya and enjoyed as a meal on its own. Locals traditionally use the leftover flesh of courgettes/zucchini that was scooped out to make the stuffed courgettes, kabak dolması. You can also use whole courgettes/zucchini as I do here to make this easy meal. Dried mint is the star spice here and its refreshing flavour complements the bulgur and courgette/zucchini. Garlic yoghurt with dried mint and cucumbers, Cacık dip, is an excellent pairing with this dish.

Method

Heat the olive oil in a heavy pan and stir in the courgette/zucchini and the onions. Cook for 3 minutes until the vegetables have softened. Add the bulgur wheat, tossing it thoroughly. Stir in the chopped tomatoes and pour in the hot water. Season with salt and ground black pepper to taste and stir to combine thoroughly.

Bring to the boil for a minute, then reduce the heat, cover and simmer for about 10-15 minutes, until all the liquid has been completely absorbed.

Turn the heat off, cover the pan with a clean dish towel and press the lid on top. Leave to steam for about 10 minutes. Then stir in the dried mint and red pepper flakes and mix with a large spoon.

You can enjoy this dish with cucumber, garlic and yoghurt, Cacık dip if you like.

Afiyet Olsun.

Bulgur & lentil pilaf with caramelised onions
Mercimekli Aş

Serves 4-6

Ingredients

225g/8oz green lentils

350g/12oz bulgur wheat, rinsed

15ml/1 tablespoon olive oil

750ml/1.3 pints hot water

*Salt and ground black pepper
to taste*

To serve:

*1 large onion, halved
and thinly sliced*

45ml/3 tablespoons olive oil

*Pickled cucumber, green or red
peppers to serve – optional*

This is a traditional dish and popular in my hometown Antakya and is so delicious with the caramelised onion slices on top. The Middle Eastern version, Mujaddara, is generally made with rice rather than bulgur.

Mercimekli Aş makes regular appearances at our dinner table and holds happy childhood memories of cooking with my mother in her kitchen. As a child, my mother would let me sauté the onions for this dish – their sweetness when caramelized complements the earthy flavour of lentils and bulgur, which I absolutely love. I like to serve Mercimekli Aş with spicy pickled peppers, biber turşusu, or a green salad with a sharp lemon juice and olive oil dressing, they accompany this dish wonderfully. Easy, healthy and delicious, Mercimekli Aş tastes even better the next day.

Method

Partially cook the green lentils in a heavy pan with plenty of hot water for about 15 minutes. Drain the water and set the green lentils aside.

Combine the partially cooked green lentils and the rinsed bulgur wheat in a heavy pan. Pour in the hot water and olive oil. Season with salt and ground black pepper to taste and stir to combine thoroughly. Bring to the boil for 1-2 minutes, and then reduce the heat. Cover and simmer until all the liquid has been completely absorbed, for about 15 minutes. Turn the heat off, cover the pan with a clean dish towel and press the lid on top. Leave to steam for about 10 minutes.

While the bulgur pilaf is cooking, heat the olive oil in a separate, heavy pan and stir in the onion slices. Over a medium heat, cook the onion slices for about 10-15 minutes until they start to get caramelized, stir occasionally. Season with salt and ground black pepper to taste.

Serve the bulgur and green lentils pilaf with the caramelized onion slices over the top. Spicy pickled cucumbers or peppers, turşu, or a green salad with a sharp lemon juice and olive oil dressing would go really well with this bulgur pilaf.

Afiyet Olsun.

Bulgur Pilaf with freekeh, aubergines/eggplants and meat
Firikli, Etli Bulgur Pilavı

Serves 6

Ingredients

350g/12oz coarse bulgur, rinsed and drained

225g/8oz firik or freekeh, rinsed and drained

1 large aubergine/eggplant, diced

2 medium onions, finely diced

450g/1lb small chunks of beef or lamb

15ml/1 tablespoon Turkish red pepper paste (biber salçası)

15ml/1 tablespoon tomato paste

60ml/2fl oz olive oil

1lt/1.75 pints hot water

Salt and ground black pepper to taste

Turkish red pepper flakes, pul biber or chili flakes to serve

Firik or freekeh is wheat that is harvested before it is ripened. The green grains are roasted and have an earthy, nutty flavour, with a similar texture to pearl barley. It is both a super grain and a time-honoured grain that has been part of Turkish and Middle Eastern cuisines for centuries.

I absolutely love freekeh's delicious, smoky taste. Freekeh used to feature a lot at my grandmother's table at our family home in Antakya, ancient Antioch. Cooked with bulgur and fresh butter, freekeh tasted divine and the tantalizing smells always greeted us when we arrived. Freekeh is a real treat by itself but also goes well with bulgur, vegetables, chickpeas and meat.

I cooked my freekeh in this recipe with bulgur, onions, aubergine/eggplant and small chunks of meat. The delicious grains worked so well with the vegetables. Please omit the meat to make the meal a vegetarian feast.

Method

First prepare the aubergine/eggplant. Peel the aubergine/eggplant lengthways in stripes using a vegetable peeler or a small sharp knife. Cut the aubergine/eggplant in quarters and then slice into bitesize pieces. Layer the pieces on a tray and sprinkle salt over them, leave them aside for 15 minutes (salt will help the moisture and bitter juices come out of the aubergine/eggplant). After 15 minutes, dry the aubergine/eggplant with kitchen or paper towel thoroughly.

Heat the 30ml/2 tablespoons of olive oil in a heavy pan and sauté the onions until soft and they begin to colour. Add the pieces of meat, stir and cook for another 1-2 minutes. Toss in the diced aubergines/eggplants and the remaining 2 tablespoons of olive oil. Stir and sauté over a medium heat for 3-4 minutes, until they start to colour and soften. Then stir in the red pepper paste and tomato paste and combine well with the vegetables and the meat. Season with salt and ground black pepper.

Now add the bulgur and freekeh to the pan and mix well. Pour in the hot water, stir and bring it to the boil. Cover, reduce the heat and simmer on a low to medium heat for about 20 minutes or until all the water has been absorbed. Turn off the heat, cover the pan with a clean kitchen towel and place the lid on firmly. Rest the pilaf for 5-10 minutes before serving.

Serve this bulgur and freekeeh pilaf hot with Turkish red pepper flakes, pul biber sprinkled over, if you like.

Afiyet Olsun.

Cabbage with bulgur, minced/ground meat and spices
Bulgurlu Lahana Kapuska

Serves 4
Ingredients

½ head of medium cabbage - 700g/1lb 9oz, washed and coarsely chopped (remove the hard stalk in the middle)

1 onion, finely chopped

225g/8oz coarse bulgur

225g/8oz minced/ground beef or lamb

15ml/1 tablespoon red pepper paste (optional)

15ml/1 tablespoon double concentrated tomato paste

Juice of ½ lemon

10ml/2 teaspoons dried mint

5ml/1 teaspoon Turkish red pepper flakes or chili flakes

570ml/1 pint hot water

30ml/2 tablespoons olive oil

Salt and ground black pepper to taste

Plain yoghurt to serve

Lahana Kapuska is a sort of deconstructed stuffed cabbage rolls; it is not only easy to make but also a great way to use up the cabbage remains when making stuffed cabbage rolls (see page 191). The name Kapuska derives from the Russian word for cabbage and this dish has many versions throughout Russia and Eastern Europe. In Turkey, there are regional variations of Kapuska too; it can be made with minced/ground meat, chunks of meat, rice or bulgur. In southern Turkey, we like to make Kapuska with bulgur, minced/ground meat, onions, flavoured with red pepper paste, biber salçası and dried mint. It is a comforting and healthy meal served with plain yoghurt. For a vegetarian version, simply omit the meat.

Method

Heat the olive oil in a large pan and stir in the minced/ground meat. Sauté for 2-3 minutes over a medium heat.

Add the onions and coarsely chopped cabbage to the pan and sauté for another 4-5 minutes (their volume will shrink as they cook).

Stir in the bulgur, tomato paste, red pepper paste (if using) and hot water. Combine well. Add the lemon juice, red pepper flakes and dried mint, season with salt and ground black pepper.

Bring to the boil, then cover and cook over a low heat for 15-20 minutes or until all is cooked. Serve hot, with extra sprinkles of dried mint and red pepper flakes and a dollop of plain yoghurt by the side.

Afiyet Olsun.

Borlotti beans with vegetables cooked in olive oil
Barbunya Pilaki

Serves 6

Ingredients

350g/12oz dried borlotti beans (or cranberry beans), soaked in warm water overnight

1 medium to large onion finely chopped

2 medium carrots, quartered and chopped in small cubes

400g/14oz/1 can of good quality chopped tomatoes

Handful of flat leaf (Italian) parsley, finely chopped

10ml/2 teaspoons sugar

45ml/3 tablespoons olive oil

570ml/1 pint water

1 lemon, cut in wedges

Salt and freshly ground black pepper to taste

Barbunya pilaki is my father's favorite Zeytinyağlı, Vegetables cooked in olive oil, Turkish style. Pilaki is a style of Turkish meze where vegetables and beans are mainly cooked with onions, garlic, tomatoes in olive oil, with a little addition of sugar, to balance the flavours. In Turkey, you can get the fresh barbunya beans (in stripy pink) or borlotti beans at the farmers' markets, pazar. It's my dad's job at my parent's home in Istanbul to pod them ready to be cooked and whoever is around joins in this therapeutic podding exercise. If you can't get hold of fresh barbunya beans, try the dried borlotti (or cranberry beans, as they are called in the USA) beans, like I have used in this recipe. This vegetarian and vegan dish is easy, delicious and packed full of goodness. Serve as part of meze spread or to accompany grills.

Note: If you are using dried borlotti (or cranberry) beans, they need to be soaked and re-hydrated in warm water for at least 8 hours or preferably overnight.

Method

Soak the dried borlotti (or cranberry) beans in warm water overnight or for at least 8 hours. Then drain the beans, rinse and transfer to a pot, filled with plenty of cold water. Bring the pot to the boil, partially cover the pot and simmer for about 30-35 minutes. Make sure the beans become tender, but not soft or mushy, they should still have a bite to them. Drain and rinse the cooked beans under cold water and set them aside.

Heat the olive oil in the pot and stir in the onions, sauté for 2-3 minutes, until they start to soften. Add the carrots, combine well and sauté for another 2 minutes.

Stir in the canned tomatoes and sugar, season with salt and freshly ground black pepper. Combine well.

Add the partially cooked beans to the pot and give it a good mix. Then pour in the water, combine well. Bring the pot to the boil; then turn the heat to low, cover the pan partially.

Simmer for 30 to 35 minutes, until the beans are cooked (but not mushy). Check the seasoning and add a little more salt or ground black pepper if needed.

Serve Barbunya Pilaki at room temperature or cold as part of a meze spread or appetizer, garnished with chopped parsley and wedges of lemon by the side to squeeze over. If you choose to serve next to main courses, I suggest serving Barbunya Pilaki warm.

Afiyet Olsun.

Bulgur and potato patties with pomegranate molasses
Bulgurlu, Patatesli Köfte

Serves 8-10

Ingredients

*175g/6oz fine bulgur,
rinsed and drained*

*4 medium potatoes,
skinned and quartered*

60ml/4 tablespoons olive oil

*3 spring onions/scallions,
finely chopped*

*Handful of flat leaf (Italian) parsley,
finely chopped*

15ml/1 tablespoon red pepper paste

*5ml/1 teaspoon Turkish red pepper
flakes or chili flakes (optional)*

10ml/2 teaspoons ground cumin

120ml/4fl oz hot water

*Salt and ground black pepper
to taste*

*Bowl of cold water to wet your
hands*

For the sauce:

*45ml/3 tablespoons extra virgin
olive oil*

*15ml/1 tablespoon pomegranate
molasses*

These bulgur and potato patties are healthy, easy to make, and so moreish, you just can't stop eating them. You can serve the patties as a meze on a bed of lettuce leaves to wrap. They are delicious dipped in olive oil and pomegranate molasses, nar ekşisi too. My family also loves to dip them into the sauce of stews and casseroles, as we do in Antakya. We use fine bulgur in these patties. But if fine bulgur is hard to find, lightly pulse coarse bulgur in a food processor for a finer consistency, taking care not to over grind (otherwise you'll have a paste). These patties can be made a day ahead - the flavours get even better the next day.

Method

In a large bowl, combine the bulgur, red pepper paste, biber salçası, red pepper flakes (if using) and spring onions/scallions, combine well using your hands. This will help the paste and the red pepper flakes to really blend in with the bulgur and the spring onions/scallions. Stir in the hot water to the mixture and give it a good mix. Leave it aside for about 15 minutes and stir once in a while so that all the water is absorbed.

Boil the potatoes in salted water until cooked, drain the water. Mash the potatoes in a separate bowl with cumin. Add the olive oil, salt and ground black pepper and knead the potatoes with your hands really well, until the potatoes are smooth and like elastic. Combine the potatoes with the bulgur mixture and add the parsley. Mix well with your hands. Check the seasoning and add more salt if needed.

Have the bowl of cold water ready by your side. Wet your hands with the water and take a walnut size piece from the mixture and shape like patties using your hands. Place them side-by-side on a serving dish.

To make the sauce; pour in the extra virgin olive oil and pomegranate molasses in a small bowl and serve the patties alongside for plunging into the sauce.

Afiyet Olsun.

Cannellini beans cooked in olive oil with vegetables
Fasulye Pilaki

Serves 4

Ingredients

400g/14oz (1 can of) cooked cannellini beans or other white beans, juice drained OR

275g/10oz dried cannellini beans or other white beans

1 medium onion, finely diced

1 medium carrot, quartered and diced in small pieces

1 medium potato, cut in small cubes

2-3 cloves of garlic, finely diced

45ml/3 tablespoons of olive oil for cooking

Handful of flat leaf (Italian) parsley, finely chopped

5ml/1 teaspoon sugar

Juice of ½ lemon

240ml/8fl oz water

Salt and freshly ground black pepper to taste

Wedges of lemon to serve

15ml/1 tablespoon of extra virgin olive oil to drizzle before serving

Fasulye Pilaki is a delicious and popular meze dish of vegetables and cannellini beans cooked with onions and garlic in olive oil. As in the case with our Zeytinyağlı dishes, vegetables are cooked in a little water and generous amount of olive oil; a little sugar can be added to balance the flavours. We serve pilaki cold or at room temperature, garnished with parsley and served with wedges of lemon. The tangy, refreshing lemon juice is a must and complements this bean-based dish very well. I love the ease of preparing this dish ahead of time; as the flavours mature, it tastes even better the next day. In addition to a meze spread, you can also serve fasulye pilaki as a side dish to grilled fish, meat or vegetables or simply enjoy on its own as a vegetarian course.

Method

If you are using dried beans, first soak the dried beans in plenty of water overnight. Next day, drain the water and boil the dried beans in fresh water for about 20 minutes, covered. Drain the water and set the partially cooked white beans aside.

If you are using pre-cooked beans from a can, simply drain its juice and rinse under cold, running water and set aside.

Heat the olive oil in the pot and stir in the onions, sauté for 2-3 minutes, until they start to soften. Then add the garlic, carrots and potato, combine well. Sauté for another 2 minutes. Pour in the water, cover and let them cook for 10 minutes on a low to medium heat.

Stir in the beans, sugar, lemon juice and season with salt and freshly ground black pepper. Combine well. Turn the heat to low, cover the pan. Simmer for another 10-15 minutes, until the beans and vegetables are cooked (but not mushy), turn the heat off. Check the seasoning and add a little more salt or ground black pepper if needed. Stir in the chopped parsley and drizzle the extra virgin olive oil over the Fasulye Pilaki, combine well. Let it cool in the pan, covered.

Serve Fasulye Pilaki at room temperature or cold as part of a meze spread or appetizer, garnished with chopped parsley and wedges of lemon by the side to squeeze over.

Afiyet Olsun.

Rice pilaf with lamb's liver, pine nuts and currants
İç Pilav

Serves 4-6

Ingredients

250g/9oz lamb's liver,
cut in bitesize pieces

30ml/2 tablespoons olive oil

15ml/1 tablespoon butter

30ml/2 tablespoons currants

45ml/3 tablespoons pine nuts

1 onion, finely chopped

10ml/2 teaspoons ground cinnamon

350g/12oz long grain rice, rinsed
and drained

750ml/1.3 pints hot water

1 small bunch of flat leaf (Italian)
parsley, finely chopped

1 small bunch of dill, finely chopped

Salt and ground black pepper

Wedges of lemon to serve

This sophisticated rice pilaf dates back to the Ottoman Palace kitchens and is packed to the brim with flavour. I love the different textures and flavours this rice showcases with currants, pine nuts as well as fresh herbs. It's been enjoyed in Istanbul, as well as in Anatolia, where you may see cubed lamb being added too. You can serve this dish on its own with a slice of lemon or with the Shepherd's salad of cucumbers, peppers and tomatoes, Çoban Salata on the side.

Method

Soak the currants in warm water for about 15 minutes.
Then drain and set aside.

Heat the butter and the olive oil in a heavy, medium size pan over a medium heat. Stir in the onion and cook for about 3 minutes, until softened. Then stir in the cubed lamb's liver and sauté for another 2 minutes to seal its juice.

Add the pine nuts and stir; as they begin to turn golden, stir in the currants, cinnamon and rice, combine well. Season with salt and ground black pepper. Pour in the hot water and bring to the boil. Then lower the heat, cover the pan and simmer gently for 15 minutes or until all the liquid has been absorbed. Turn off the heat, cover the pan with a clean kitchen towel and place the lid back on tightly. Leave to steam for 10 minutes.

Just before serving, stir in the chopped parsley and dill and combine gently. Serve with wedges of lemon by the side.

Afiyet Olsun.

Oval bulgur balls with walnuts and minced/ground meat
Oruk

(Makes 5 Oruk, oval stuffed bulgur balls and a tray baked sini oruk, in 32cm/about 12in round baking dish)

Serves 12-14
Ingredients
For the filling:

250g/9oz minced/ground beef (medium fat)

100g/4oz shelled walnuts, finely crushed to small, bite size pieces

3 medium onions, finely grated

1 small bunch of flat leaf (Italian) parsley, finely chopped

30ml/2 tablespoons olive oil

10ml/2 teaspoons ground black pepper

10ml/2 teaspoons Turkish red pepper flakes, pul biber or chili flakes

Salt to taste (at least 10ml/2 teaspoons recommended)

For the bulgur dough:

450g/1lb fine bulgur, köftelik bulgur

360ml/12fl oz warm water to wet the bulgur and 240ml/8fl oz warm water to knead the bulgur

170g/6oz coarse semolina

120ml/4fl oz warm water (for semolina)

250g/9oz extra lean (double grinded) minced/ground beef

60ml/4 tablespoons red pepper paste, biber salçası

15ml/1 tablespoon ground cumin

10ml/2 teaspoons Turkish red pepper flakes, pul biber or chili flakes

Salt to taste

Bowl of cold water for shaping the oval bulgur balls

Oruk, or Şam Oruğu as this dish is often called, are oval-shaped bulgur balls baked with a minced/ground meat and walnut filling. It is a popular dish in my hometown, Antakya and it is still a special dish my mother makes for festive events and family gatherings.

Antakya's Oruk is a variation of the Middle Eastern kibbeh. The difference being the spices and some ingredients used (Kibbeh typically uses allspice and pine nuts) as well as the cooking method (Oruk is baked whereas kibbeh is generally fried). Whenever we go back home, Oruk is part of the welcome back home dinner on our first night with my mother's other speciality dishes like Mevlübi; the layers of rice with aubergine/eggplant, meat, onion and potatoes and Cevizli Biber; walnut and red pepper paste dip. Surrounded by my mother's lovingly home-cooked food and the company of family and friends, we always know we are back home.

Making Oruk is a grand event at home; I grew up watching my grandmother and mother making this special treat with our extended family gathered around the big table in her 450-year-old home in Antakya. Some would make the filling, some prepared the bulgur dough and some did the stuffing. A real, earthy, production line. Since there were no food processors around in those days, they would ground the meat and bulgur with hand held machines. There were lots of kneading and mixing involved and since they would make vast amounts to share, it would almost take a day for this feast to get ready.

A few tips here to ease the process. I suggest that you prepare the filling a day in advance, if you have limited time. The filling anyway needs to be cool and this really helps with spreading the work. To keep the bulgur dough to stay intact, semolina is the key; it works great as the binding agent in the bulgur dough. You also need to have water aside and continuously wet your hands while shaping the dough. Minced/ground meat that goes in the bulgur dough needs to be extra lean and double grinded (you may ask your butcher to do this for you or you can pulse the minced/ground meat in your food processor a few times). You may also like to make the easier Sini Oruk; tray baked bulgur spread with minced/ground meat and stuffing in the middle. They are both very special treats, almost sacred food for us and worth all the effort.

Recipe continues on to the next page...

Oval bulgur balls with walnuts and minced/ground meat
Oruk

Method

Preheat the oven to 160°C/320°F/Gas Mark 3

Grease a baking tray for the oval bulgur balls and a 32cm/12in round baking dish for the tray bake oruk version, if you prefer to make this version too.

First make the filling, as it needs to cool down (to save time and to spread the work, you can also prepare the filling a day in advance and keep in the fridge, covered). Heat the oil in a heavy pan and stir in the minced/ground beef (medium fat). Sauté and stir the meat, breaking the lumps into smaller pieces, over a medium heat for about 8-10 minutes, until all the juice has evaporated. Add the grated onion, salt, ground black pepper and red pepper flakes and sauté for another 5–8 minutes until the onions are softened and begin to colour. Then add the finely crushed walnuts and the chopped parsley, mix well and turn the heat off. Leave aside to cool down. (This really is a delicious filling, and any leftovers would make a great pasta sauce).

Now, let's make the bulgur dough. Place the fine bulgur in a large mixing bowl (big enough for you to be able to knead). Stir in the red pepper paste, cumin, salt and red pepper flakes and using your hands, mix them all well. Then slowly pour the 360ml/12fl oz warm water all over it. Again using your hands, give the bulgur mixture a good mix and make sure all the bulgur is wet. Let it rest and absorb the water for 10 minutes. In the meantime, place the semolina in a separate bowl and stir in the 120ml/4fl oz warm water over it. Using your hands, knead and turn the semolina mixture into a soft dough. Semolina is important here as it helps with binding the bulgur dough.

Have the warm water bowl (for kneading the bulgur) next to you and start kneading the mixture for about 5 minutes. Wet your hands with the water continuously while kneading. Stir in the semolina dough into this bulgur mixture and wetting your hands, knead for another 5 minutes, you will see that the dough is getting more like elastic and binding together. Add the double grinded extra lean beef to the mixture (you can use your food processor to grind the meat) and again with wet hands, knead for 10 minutes, until you get a smooth, elastic dough.

Now, have a bowl of cold water at the side to shape the oval bulgur balls, and to avoid the bulgur dough sticking to your hands and for the balls to stay intact. Wet your hands with the cold water and take a small tangerine size bulgur dough into your palm. Roll it into an oval shape and then using your thumb, hollow out an opening in the middle. Shape the ball into a thin-walled (about 0.6cm/¼in thick) oval with an opening at one end by moulding the ball around your finger, gradually tapering the closed end. Mend any cracks in the shell with a moistened finger. Fill the bulgur shell with about 1½ tablespoons of the filling.

Moisten edges of the opening, then pinch the edges of the ball to seal. Wet your hands and gently form the stuffed bulgur ball into the shape of an oval with slightly pointy edges. Place it on an oiled tray. Repeat the same shaping with remaining filling and bulgur dough. (The quantities here makes 5 Oruk, oval stuffed bulgur balls and a tray baked sini oruk, in 32cm/ about 12in round baking dish. Alternatively, you can make about 18 oval Oruk balls in total if you prefer). Place all the finished oval bulgur balls in a well-oiled baking tray and coat them all with olive oil.

Bake the oval shaped Oruk balls in the preheated oven for about 35-40 minutes, until it has a crispy and golden brown topping. Bulgur absorbs olive oil quickly, so coat oval bulgur balls with extra olive oil towards the end, so they won't crack.

You can serve Şam Oruk, oval bulgur balls warm.

Afiyet Olsun.

Tray bake bulgur spread with minced/ground meat and walnut filling
Sini Oruğu

Serves 4-6

Makes a tray baked sini oruk, in 32cm/about 12in round baking dish

Ingredients (as stated in Oruk recipe, page 227)

Sini Oruk is another type of baked içli köfte and this tray baked version is much easier. If you prefer, make 5 oval bulgur balls as explained in the oval bulgur balls with walnuts and minced/ground meat recipe and then make a tray bake version with the remaining ingredients, as I prefer to do here.

Method

Grease a 32cm/12in round baking dish (or equivalent size) for the tray bake oruk.

To make it, divide the remaining of your bulgur dough into two. Grease a (preferably) round baking dish of 32cm/12in diameter with 2 tablespoons of olive oil. Wetting your hands with cold water, spread a thin layer of half of the bulgur dough onto the oiled baking dish. Make sure the spread stays intact; wet your hands and seal any broken parts of the sphere. Spread the minced/ground meat and walnut filling evenly over the bulgur dough spread, press gently.

Grease a chopping board or a work surface with 1 tablespoon of olive oil. Take a handful of the remaining bulgur dough and spread with your hands to form a thin layer (about $\frac{1}{3}$ cm). Place this stretched bulgur dough onto the filling over the round baking dish. Continue until you finish the dough and the top layer is covered, like a patchwork. Wet your hands and bind all the loose ends (you need to prepare the top layer on another oiled surface so that you won't press too hard over the filling and break it into parts).

Oil the top layer of the bulgur spread, with about 2 tablespoons of olive oil and cut into diamond or triangle shaped slices.

Bake the Sini Oruk in the preheated oven at 160°C/320°F/Gas Mark 3 for about 35-40 minutes, until it has a crispy and golden brown topping. Bulgur absorbs olive oil quickly, so coat the tray bake Sini Oruk with extra olive oil towards the end, so it won't crack.

Once cooked, it is best to wait for the Sini Oruk to cool down for 10-15 minutes so that it won't break apart.

Afiyet Olsun.

Chapter Ten

Fish & Seafood

Fish & Seafood

Turkey's coastline borders the Black Sea, Aegean Sea and the Mediterranean providing its flourishing fishing industry with a wide variety of fish and seafood from: sea bass, mackerel, sardines, anchovies, mullet and swordfish. To retain freshness and flavour, we Turks prepare fish simply with a brush of olive oil and usually cooked over a grill. Served with a simple salad, for me, this dish epitomizes long summer evenings on the Turkish coast, dining in the open air.

A popular Turkish street food is grilled or lightly fried fish sandwich called Balık Ekmek. From small coastal fishing towns to the harbour docks in Istanbul, fishermen grill their day's catch by their boat and sell this delicious sandwich snack. With a warm breeze from the Bosphorus and a view of boats in the harbour, that first bite is a true taste of home for me. Turkish spirit, rakı, made of twice-distilled grapes and aniseed is a popular and traditional drink to accompany seafood in Turkey.

I like cooking fish with vegetables at home; such as the baked sea bass with vegetables in olive oil – Fırında Sebzeli Levrek. It makes a complete, easy, healthy dinner.

Baked prawns with onions, peppers, mushroom and tomatoes
Karides Güveç

Serves 4

Ingredients

225g/8oz fresh raw king prawns/ jumbo shrimp, shelled, cleaned and pat dried

225g/8oz chestnut mushrooms, wiped cleaned, halved and sliced

1 onion, quartered and thinly sliced

3 garlic cloves, chopped

1 green bell pepper (or 2 sivri biber, pointy pepper, if you can get), seeded, quartered and thinly sliced

2 bay leaves (optional)

400g/14oz good quality 1 can of chopped tomatoes

120g/4oz grated cheddar (or kasar) or mozzarella, if you prefer a milder taste

45ml/3 tablespoons olive oil

60ml/2fl oz water

Salt and freshly ground black pepper to taste

10ml/2 teaspoons red pepper flakes, Turkish pul biber or chili flakes

Handful of chopped flat leaf (Italian) parsley, for garnish

Slices of fresh, crusty bread or Turkish flat breads, pide bread to serve

This popular one pot dish is served in fish restaurants throughout Turkey as a hot meze. Traditionally, prawns are cooked with plenty of vegetables in one big earthenware pot (or small individual pots), called güveç (if you don't have one, a ramekin dish or a glass baking dish also works very well). The combination of tomatoes, mushrooms, onions, peppers and garlic baked together in olive oil with the prawns is irresistible. Serve Karides Güveç as an appetizer or larger portions make a satisfying main course with crusty or pide bread to soak up the flavourful juices.

Method

Preheat oven to 180°C/350°F/Gas Mark 4

Heat the olive oil in a wide, heavy pan over medium heat. Stir in the onion, peppers and mushrooms and cook for about 4-5 minutes, until they begin to soften. Add the garlic, season with salt (mushrooms especially require generous seasoning) ground black pepper and red pepper flakes, pul biber. Stir and cook over a medium heat for another 4-5 minutes. Add the chopped tomatoes, bay leaves and water, combine well. Simmer over a medium to low heat for about 10 minutes, until you get a nice chunky sauce. Check the seasoning of your sauce and add more salt or spices to your taste.

Stir in the fresh, raw king prawns/jumbo shrimp to the sauce and mix well. Spoon this mixture into individual or one big earthenware pot or ramekin dish or any baking dish you have. Sprinkle the grated cheese over the top and bake in the preheated oven for about 10 minutes or until the king prawns/jumbo shrimp are just cooked through and the cheese is nicely golden brown on top.

Garnish with chopped parsley over the top and serve hot with slices of crusty bread or Turkish flat breads, pide bread by the side.

Afiyet Olsun.

Mussels stuffed with aromatic rice
Midye Dolma

Makes 25-30 stuffed mussels

Ingredients

25-30 large black mussels, cleaned and bearded

2 medium to large onions, finely chopped

30g/1oz currants

30g/1oz pine nuts

110g/3¾ oz short grain rice

1 tomato, very finely chopped or grated

Handful of chopped flat leaf (Italian) parsley, for garnish

Handful of finely chopped fresh dill

15ml/1 tablespoon tomato paste

5ml/1 teaspoon ground black pepper

5ml/1 teaspoon Turkish red pepper flakes or chili flakes

5ml/1 teaspoon ground cinnamon

60ml/2fl oz olive oil

240ml/8fl oz hot water

Salt to taste

Lemon wedges to serve

Midye Dolma, stuffed mussels are a favourite street and beachside food in Turkey. Our summer family holidays are often spent in Bodrum, where we enjoy platefuls of these freshly stuffed mussels from a local vendor. My 13-year-old son is particularly fond of these mussels and can devour a small plate of them on his own! You can also find freshly prepared midye dolma on street stalls in Istanbul, especially in the Beyoğlu district. Gently break off the top shell, add a good squeeze of lemon juice over the mussels then using the loose shell as a spoon, scoop out the rice and mussel to enjoy.

Some important tips on making stuffed mussels, midye dolma at home:

1. Opening the shell of the live mussels may seem a little challenging at first; soaking them in warm water helps to open the shell, as it relaxes the mussels. Make sure to discard any broken or open shells. Tap any half-open shells; do not use any that do not close immediately.

2. The herby, aromatic rice itself is really delicious and you can make it ahead of time. I make mine the day beforehand and keep it in the fridge, covered; it really helps for the flavours to settle.

3. Plenty of onions in the aromatic rice really go well; they pack a lot of flavour combined with currants, pine nuts, herbs and spices. I like to add a little red pepper flakes to bring a delicious but not overpowering heat to the mussels.

4. Try not to overstuff the mussels with the aromatic rice, as the rice will need a little space to cook further.

Making stuffed mussels at home is a labour of love but so rewarding, well worth the effort. This recipe is slightly adapted from Somer Sivrioğlu and David Dale's wonderful Turkish cookery book, Anatolia, Adventures in Turkish Cooking.

Recipe continues on to the next page...

Mussels stuffed with aromatic rice
Midye Dolma

Method

Place the currants in a bowl, cover with warm water and soak for 15 minutes. Then drain and set aside. Place the rice into a sieve and rinse well under cold running water. Drain the rice and set aside.

Make the stuffing first (you can also make the stuffing a day ahead). Heat the oil in a medium-sized pan and stir in the onions. Sauté over a medium to high heat for 5 minutes.

Stir in the pine nuts to the onions, sauté over a medium heat for 3 minutes, stirring often. Add the rice, currants, chopped tomato, tomato paste, spices and season with salt to your taste. Pour in 240ml/8fl oz of hot water and combine all well. Bring to the boil then cover to simmer over a low heat for 15 minutes, until all the liquid has been absorbed. The rice will still have a bite to it. Remove from the heat and leave to cool.

Once cool, stir in the chopped dill and parsley to the aromatic rice and combine well. Check the seasoning and add more salt or ground black pepper if you want to. Set aside to cool.

Now, open the mussels. If you've bought the mussels in a vacuum-packed bag, open the bag over a bowl to catch any liquid inside. Place the mussels in a large bowl and rinse under cold water. Scrub the shells clean and scrape off any dirt. Using a blunt knife, carefully force the point of the knife into the gap at the pointy end of each mussel. Slice through the meat so the shell opens with half the meat attached to each half shell – once you cut through the thick, round connecting muscle at the bottom of the mussel, it will be easy to open.

Pour the juice from the mussel to a bowl. Snip off the beards and using your finger, remove any grit at the base. Spread the half shells to tear the muscle of the mussel, but leave the two halves connected. Put about 2 teaspoons of stuffing into the middle of each mussel (try not to overfill) and push the half shells together again.

Place the mussels on a wide heavy pan, with the tips pointing outwards towards the edge of the pan, with the shells slightly overlapping (to prevent them opening). Build a tight spiral of shells in the centre of the pan. There should be one layer of mussels, so if you have mussels left over, use another pan to keep on the one level layering. Place a wide plate over the mussels to prevent them from opening too wide while they cook.

Strain the mussel juice through a sieve lined with a double layer of muslin/cheese cloth three times to remove any grit. Mix the mussel juice with water, make it up about 270ml/9fl oz of water. Pour this mixture to the pan; the water level should only reach to the half of the shell. Cover the pan and bring to the boil, then reduce the heat and simmer for 15 minutes.

Remove the mussels from the heat and leave to cool at room temperature. Then cover and keep them in the fridge for 30-60 minutes to cool further and for the flavours to settle. Serve stuffed mussels with aromatic rice, midye dolma on a big platter with lemon wedges by the side. They are best enjoyed eating with your hands, using the top shell to scoop the mixture out of the bottom shell, with a generous squeeze of lemon over the mussel with aromatic rice.

Afiyet Olsun.

Poached anchovies with vegetables
Hamsi Buğulama

Serves 4

Ingredients

450g/1lb anchovies, filleted

2 medium potatoes, cut in half and thinly sliced

2 medium tomatoes, thinly sliced

1 onion, cut in half and thinly sliced

3 spring (green) onions/scallions, finely chopped

1 lemon, thinly sliced

Handful of flat leaf (Italian) parsley, finely chopped

45ml/3 tablespoons olive oil

120ml/4fl oz water

Salt and ground black pepper to taste

Turkish red pepper flakes or chili flakes to taste (optional)

This small, oily fish, called hamsi, is much loved in Turkish cuisine, especially in towns along the Black Sea coast. There are many anchovy recipes celebrating this delicious little fish at Turkey's Black Sea region. I prefer the simple method of poaching these intensely flavoured anchovy fillets with layers of fresh vegetables in a little water and olive oil. This method of cooking is called buğulama (steamed) in Turkish cuisine. It is healthy and also retains the juices of each ingredient. I like how the tomatoes, potatoes, and onions in this dish balance the strong fishy flavour of anchovies. I add slices of lemon and chopped parsley for their sharp refreshing taste to finish off this one pot meal. Small white fish and sardines are a good substitute for anchovies. You may be able to get your anchovies gutted and cleaned by a skilled fishmonger or buy as fillets.

Method

Combine the onions, spring onions/scallions, parsley and 30ml/2 tablespoons olive oil in a large bowl. Season with salt, ground black pepper and red pepper flakes (if using). Knead well with your hands to infuse the spices to the onion; this will also soften them and release their juice.

Parboil (partially cook) the potatoes in a pan of boiling water for 5-7 minutes then drain the water. Stir in the parboiled potatoes to the onion mixture and gently combine well.

Pour in the remaining olive oil to a wide, heavy pan. Layer and spread the onions and potatoes in the pan.

Lay the anchovy fillets evenly on top of onions and potatoes. Next, layer the slices of tomatoes and lemon over the fish. Season with salt and ground black pepper to your taste.

Pour in the water to the pan. Cover and start cooking over a medium heat until it starts to bubble. Then lower the heat and cook for 15-20 minutes (depending on the size of the fish), or until the fish and vegetables are cooked.

Serve hot with some crusty bread at the side if you like.

Afiyet Olsun.

Mackerel with sumac salad on bread
Balık Ekmek

Serves 4

Ingredients

*4 fillets of mackerel
(or white fish of your choice)*

15ml/1 tablespoon olive oil

*Salt and ground black pepper
to taste*

*Turkish somun bread (traditional
loaf) or bread rolls to serve*

**For red onion, tomato and
parsley salad with sumac:**

*½ red onion, cut in half
and thinly sliced*

3 medium tomatoes, finely chopped

*Handful of flat leaf (Italian) parsley,
finely chopped*

*30ml/2 tablespoons extra virgin
olive oil*

Juice of ½ lemon

5ml/1 teaspoon ground sumac

*Sea salt and ground black pepper
to taste*

One of the most popular street foods at home is grilled (or lightly fried) fish, served on our traditional white loaf, somun ekmek. Fishermen grill the fish at their boats and prepare this sandwich right there for you. Whenever I am in Eminönü, Istanbul, I always stop by the fishermen to get my Balık Ekmek; with the view of traditional ferries passing by, it is always a special moment to pause, reflect and enjoy this treat.

Depending on what is seasonally available, mackerel, sea bass or bonito will all work with this recipe. I serve my Balık Ekmek with a refreshing, tangy sumac salad as it pairs with the grilled fish beautifully.

Method

For the sumac salad; combine a pinch of salt and sumac into the onion slices with your hands really well in a bowl. This will soften the onions and make them more palatable. Let the sumac really penetrate into the onions. Add the chopped tomatoes, parsley, lemon juice and extra virgin olive oil into the bowl and combine well. Season with ground black pepper; your salad is ready.

To cook the fish; place a wide, heavy grill pan on a medium heat. Brush the fish fillets with olive oil on both sides, then season with salt and freshly ground black pepper.

Quarter the traditional somun bread and slice them in the middle, or slice the bread rolls.

When the grill is hot, place the fish skin side down and cook for 2-3 minutes (please refer to the packaging of the fish of your choice for cooking instructions and time). The colour will turn from transparent to opaque; then, turn over and cook for 1-2 minutes on the other side, until the fish is fully cooked. Turn the heat off.

Place the cooked fish on the bread pockets (or on the rolls) and then place a spoonful of the sumac salad over them.

Afiyet Olsun.

Baked sea bass with vegetables in olive oil
Fırında Sebzeli Levrek

Serves 4

Ingredients

4 fillets of sea bass – or any fresh white fish of your choice*

1 onion, cut in half and sliced thinly

4-6 cloves of garlic, crushed and chopped coarsely

1 small green (bell or pointy) pepper, quartered and sliced thinly

1 small yellow (bell or pointy) pepper, quartered and sliced thinly

3 medium tomatoes, coarsely sliced

2 medium potatoes, cut in half and thinly sliced

Juice of 1 lemon

2 bay leaves

240ml/8fl oz water (or fish stock)

45ml/3 tablespoons olive oil

5ml/1 teaspoon red pepper flakes – optional

Salt and ground black pepper to taste

Handful of flat leaf (Italian) parsley, coarsely chopped – to decorate

Lemon wedges to serve

Sea bass is another popular fish in Turkish cuisine and this delicious fish course appears at our family table often. I poach the sea bass and vegetables in olive oil, lemon juice and a little water to make this easy one-pot meal. This is a healthy way of cooking as the flavourful juices of both the fish and vegetables are retained.

This recipe is inspired by Süreyya Üzmez, an acclaimed food journalist, seafood expert and owner of the Trilye fish restaurant in Ankara, the capital of Turkey. I had the pleasure of being a part of his TV programme, Turkish Chefs of the World, aired on TRT, Turkish National Television, as well as in 37 other countries. I adapted this recipe from his cookbook Trilye's Passion for Sea Food, Trilye'nin Balık Sevdası.

Method

*Please check the recommended cooking time for the fish of your choice on the packaging.

Preheat the oven to 180°C/350°F/Gas Mark 4

Stir in all the prepared vegetables and the bay leaves in a baking dish. Coat them with 30ml/2 tablespoons of olive oil, salt, ground black pepper and red pepper flakes (if used).

Coat the fish fillets with the remaining 15ml/1 tablespoon of olive oil and place them among the vegetables. Mix the lemon juice with water or fish stock and spoon this liquid all around the fish and vegetables. Cover the baking dish with foil and put it in the oven for about 35 minutes or until the fish and vegetables are cooked. Once cooked, take the foil off and sprinkle chopped parsley over the fish. Serve immediately with wedges of lemon by the side.

Afiyet Olsun.

Fish kebabs with roasted vegetables
Sebzeli Balık Şiş

Serves 2-3

Ingredients

350g/12oz skinned, boneless cod loin (or any firm fleshed fish), cut into bite size chunks

1 red onion, quartered and coarsely sliced

1 red and 1 green pointy (or bell) peppers, de-seeded and coarsely sliced

1 lemon, cut into small wedges

5-6 fresh bay leaves

30ml/2 tablespoons olive oil (for roasting the vegetables)

For the marinade:

30ml/2 tablespoons olive oil

Juice of ½ lemon

5ml/1 teaspoon Turkish red pepper flakes or chili flakes

Salt and freshly ground black pepper to taste

Lemon wedges to serve

This tasty fish kebab is easy to prepare with any firm fleshed fish such as cod, tuna or salmon. Meaty swordfish, kılıç balığı, is traditionally used to make fish kebabs in Turkey as its firm, dense flesh holds together well. I often roast extra vegetables in the same dish by the side to complement the fish kebabs. Served with boiled potatoes on the side, these fish kebabs make a delicious and impressive meal for entertaining.

Note: It is worth marinating the fish prior to cooking; a simple marinade of olive oil, refreshing lemon juice with a little spicy kick from red pepper flakes flavour the fish kebabs beautifully. Soak wooden skewers in water for 15 minutes before using.

Method

Preheat oven to 180°C/350°F/Gas Mark 4

Cut the skinned, boneless cod loin (or your choice of firm fleshed fish) into bite size (about 1.18in/3 cm) chunks.

Place the fish in a bowl and stir in the olive oil, lemon juice and red pepper flakes. Season the fish with salt and ground black pepper. Gently coat the chunks of the fish with this marinade. Cover the bowl and set aside for 15 minutes to marinate and for the fish to absorb the flavours.

Place the chopped red onion, red pointy (or bell) pepper and green pepper slices on a baking tray. Drizzle 30ml/2 tablespoons of olive oil over them. Season with salt, ground black pepper and mix well.

Thread the fish on to the skewers, alternating with a wedge of lemon, red onion slice, red and green pepper slices. Thread one or two bay leaves into each skewer. Brush the kebabs with any leftover marinade.

Place the skewers at one side of your baking tray. Spread the remaining chopped vegetables next to the fish kebab skewers. Bake in the preheated oven for 20-25 minutes (please refer to the cooking instructions on the packaging for the fish of your choice).

Serve the fish kebabs hot with roasted vegetables and a wedge of lemon by the side. Boiled or roasted potatoes also complement the fish kebabs well.

Afiyet Olsun.

Grilled sardines in vine leaves with vegetables
Sebzeli Izgara Sardalya

Serves 4-5

Ingredients

250g/10oz sardines (12 pieces), scaled, gutted and washed

1 green, red or yellow bell (or pointy) pepper (or mixture), cut in half and sliced in long strips

10-12 cherry tomatoes, halved

Juice of ½ lemon

12 preserved vine leaves

30ml/2 tablespoons olive oil

5ml/1 teaspoon Turkish red pepper flakes or chili flakes

Salt and ground black pepper to taste

Wedges of lemon to serve

Handful of fresh dill, coarsely chopped to decorate

Grilled (or chargrilled) sardines are especially popular during the balmy summer months in Turkey. Sardines are often wrapped in vine leaves and then grilled. The sharp, tangy taste of vine leaves balance the strong flavour of sardines. Preserved vine leaves sold in jars are mostly available in supermarkets or Middle Eastern and Mediterranean stores.

I grill my sardines with small cherry tomatoes and bell peppers to add another layer of juicy, sweet flavours. Serve these sardines with wedges of lemon.

Method

Heat the olive oil in a pan and sauté the bell peppers for 3-4 minutes. Toss the tomatoes into the pan and mix them well. Season with salt and ground black pepper and add the red pepper flakes. Mix them well and turn the heat off.

Spread the vine leaves out on a flat surface and place a sardine on each leaf. Wrap each sardine loosely in the leaf like a cigar. Brush each leaf with a little olive oil and place seam side down.

Place the sardines on a baking tray. Spread the tomato and bell pepper mixture among the sardines. Squeeze half a lemon over the mixture.

Preheat the grill on medium to high heat. Place the tray under the grill and cook for 3-4 minutes each side, until the fish is cooked and vine leaves are charred. Once cooked, sprinkle the fresh dill all over and serve hot, with wedges of lemon by the side.

Afiyet Olsun.

Chapter Eleven

Desserts

Sweet Treats & Turkish Coffee

Desserts, sweet treats and Turkish coffee

Turks are known for their sweet tooth and meals will invariably end with a dessert or fresh fruit. My dear brother-in-law, Mehmet, will rearrange his dinner making dessert the main event! Desserts also play an important role in Turkish culture and are the centre piece at religious festivals, weddings and family celebrations.

I am especially partial to fruit-based desserts such as dried apricots baked with walnuts, Cevizli kuru kayısı tatlısı. It is light and packed with a sweet and nutty flavour. Homemade Baklava is a special treat and my version is fragrant, lemony and lighter than its commercially available versions. This chapter also includes southern Turkish specialities such as Künefe, Kadayifi and one of the nation's hallmarks, Turkish delight, Lokum.

A Turkish meal draws to a close with coffee - no ordinary coffee… but Turkish coffee, Türk kahvesi, or tea, çay.

I hope you enjoy recreating some of Turkey's sweet delights in this chapter.

Syrup soaked, cheese filled pastry strands
Künefe

Serves 6

Ingredients

225g/8oz shredded kadayif - künefe pastry strands, thawed if frozen

145g/5oz melted unsalted butter

300g/12oz fresh mozzarella, sliced (or Antakya's white cheese for künefe, künefelik peynir or dil peyniri in Turkey if you can get it)

45ml/3 tablespoons kaymak or clotted cream – optional

For the syrup:

225g/8oz granulated sugar

120ml/4fl oz water

Juice of ½ small lemon

30ml/2 tablespoons crushed pistachios for garnish (optional)

This glorious baked pastry strands in syrup called künefe is a signature dessert from my hometown, Antakya. The actual pastry strands can also be referred as künefe or kadayif. I remember as a child watching the delicate pastry strands being squeezed through a huge sieve at our local künefe shop in Long Market, Uzun Çarşı. My grandmother would prepare Künefe in her garden as we waited excitedly for any leftovers of buttery soaked pastry strands.

Tel kadayif is a dough, pushed through a sieve to form delicate strands, which looks like vermicelli noodles and when soaked in butter and baked, resembles golden shredded wheat. It is the basis for many desserts but, in my opinion, this is the most impressive. There is a particular unsalted cheese called beyaz künefelik peynir we use for künefe in Antakya. Unsalted fresh mozzarella will work just as well. I also like to add a little clotted cream to the filling (or kaymak, Turkish thick cream from water buffaloes, if available). Künefe can be baked in one large pan or as smaller individual portions. Künefe or kadayif pastry strands are available at Turkish and Middle Eastern food stores.

Method

Preheat oven to 180°C/350°F/Gas Mark 4

First make the syrup. Place the sugar and water in a pan and simmer over a low to medium heat until the sugar is dissolved. Stir in the lemon juice and simmer for about 15 minutes, until the syrup coats the back of the spoon. Then remove from the heat and leave the syrup to cool. It is essential that the syrup needs to be cool when poured over the cheese filled pastry strands.

Using some of the melted butter, grease a large baking tray.

Soak the pastry strands well in the melted butter. Use more butter if necessary, as it is important that the pastry is well soaked in order to prevent it burning during baking. Divide the pastry strands in two. Spread half of the strands in the base of the baking pan, press it down with your fingers.

Spread or crumble the slices of the fresh mozzarella cheese and the clotted cream or kaymak (if used) over the top of the pastry. Then cover with the remainder of the pastry, pressing down firmly.

Bake the pastry in the preheated oven for 35-40 minutes or until the strands are a deep golden colour.

Cut the hot, baked pastry strands into portions and pour the prepared cool syrup over it. Serve immediately while still hot and the cheese is gooey. You can decorate künefe with a sprinkling of ground pistachio nuts over the top if you like.

Afiyet Olsun.

Baklava with pistachios and walnuts
Fıstıklı ve Cevizli Baklava

Serves 12

Ingredients

230g/8oz melted unsalted butter

440g/1lb (2 packs of) filo pastry sheets – total 24 sheets – thawed

400g/14oz walnuts, finely chopped

10ml/2 teaspoons ground cinnamon

For the syrup:

450g/1lb sugar

420ml/14fl oz water

Juice of 1 lemon

12inx7in/30cmx19cm baking dish to bake

To serve:

Ground pistachio nuts to sprinkle over the baklavas

Baklava is a legacy of the Ottoman Empire and was perfected by the pastry chefs in the Topkapı Palace. Baklava is enjoyed as a mid-morning sweet snack with Turkish coffee or tea, or as a mid-afternoon treat and as a dessert after lunch or dinner. Any time of day works for a good piece of baklava! The real thing shouldn't be overly sweet and heavy, but light enough to tempt you to eat a small plateful of these flaky delicacies. I like this fragrant and lighter version than the commercially available baklavas. Filo pastry sheets work well for making homemade baklava and it's easier than you think. This recipe is adapted from Ghillie Başan's The Complete Book of Turkish Cooking.

Method

Preheat oven to 160°C/325°F/Gas Mark 3

Make the syrup first. Put the sugar into a heavy pan, pour in water and bring to the boil, stirring all the time. When the sugar is dissolved, lower the heat and stir in the lemon juice. Then simmer for about 15 minutes, until the syrup thickens. Leave to cool in the pan.

Melt the butter in a small pan and then brush a little over the bottom and sides of the baking pan.

Place two sheets of filo pastry in the bottom of the greased pan and brush it with melted butter (trim from the edges to fit, if needed). Continue until you have used 12 filo sheets, brushing every two sheets with butter. Ease the sheets into the corners and trim the edges if they flop over the rim of the pan.

Spread the walnuts over the twelfth buttered sheet and sprinkle with the cinnamon, and then continue as before with the remaining filo sheets. Brush the top one as well, then, using a sharp knife cut diagonal parallel lines right through all the layers to the bottom to form small diamond shapes.

Bake the baklava in the preheated oven for about 45 minutes or until the top is golden – if it is still pale, increase the temperature for a few minutes.

When the baklava is ready, remove it from the oven and slowly pour the cooled syrup over the piping hot pastry. Return to the oven for 2-3 minutes to soak up the syrup, then take it out and leave to cool.

Once the baklava is cool, gently lift the diamond shaped pieces out of the pan and arrange them onto a serving plate. Serve baklava pieces with ground pistachios over them, always at room temperature.

Note: Baklava should never be stored in the refrigerator, as the fat congeals, pastry absorbs in the moisture and it becomes soggy.

Afiyet Olsun.

Zesty semolina sponge cake in syrup
Revani

Serves 6-8

Ingredients

165g/6oz coarse semolina

200g/7oz sugar

45ml/3 tablespoons all-purpose/ plain flour

5ml/1 teaspoon baking powder

225g/8oz plain whole milk yoghurt

3 medium eggs, beaten

60ml/4 tablespoons light olive oil

10ml/2 teaspoons vanilla extract

Zest of 1 lemon

Juice of ½ lemon

For the syrup:

300g/10 ½ oz sugar

360ml/12fl oz water

Juice of ½ lemon

Ground pistachio nuts and desiccated coconut to serve

Revani is a deliciously moist semolina sponge cake in light syrup, very popular at my Turkish cookery classes. It is easy to make, light and fluffy in texture - a real crowd pleaser. Revani has been a popular dessert with Turks since the Ottoman period. It is believed this dessert was named Revani when the Ottomans conquered the city of Yerevan in today's Armenia. Revani has many variations and is enjoyed especially in the Eastern Mediterranean countries including Turkey. Rose water, orange flower water, or orange zest can also be added to Revani for a natural delicate flavouring. Revani is often decorated with ground pistachios or desiccated coconut and served with a cup of çay or Türk kahvesi.

Method

Preheat oven to 180°C/350°F/Gas Mark 4

First make the syrup, as it needs to cool down. Combine the sugar and water in a medium saucepan at a medium heat. Stir and bring the mixture to the boil. Once it boils, reduce the heat to low and let the syrup simmer for about 10 minutes, uncovered. Add the lemon juice, mix well and simmer for another 5 minutes. Turn the heat off and let the syrup cool down while you make the semolina cake.

Grease a square or rectangular baking dish 8in x 10in/20cm x 27cm with 2 tablespoons of olive oil. Beat the eggs and combine with the sugar in a large mixing bowl. Beat and combine well for a few minutes, until the sugar dissolves. Then add the remaining 2 tablespoons of olive oil, yoghurt, semolina, flour, the baking powder and beat well. Stir in the vanilla extract, lemon juice and lemon zest and mix well until you have a smooth batter. Pour the batter into the greased baking dish and bake in the preheated oven for about 30-35 minutes, until the cake is golden brown. To check; insert a toothpick into the centre of the cake, if it comes out clean, that means the cake is cooked. If not, bake for another 3-5 minutes.

Using a large spoon, drizzle the cooled syrup all over the semolina cake. Let the cake absorb the syrup and cool down. Once cool, cut the Revani in square or diamond shapes; you can serve Revani with ground pistachio and desiccated coconut over the top like we do back home.

Afiyet Olsun.

Dried baked apricots with walnuts
Cevizli Kuru Kayısı Tatlısı

Serves 4-6

Ingredients

225g/8oz dried (Turkish) apricots

30ml/2 tablespoons unsalted butter

15ml/1 tablespoon brown sugar

For the filling:

*85g/3oz walnuts,
crushed into small pieces*

30g/1oz brown sugar

120ml/4fl oz water for baking

Crushed pistachio nuts for garnish

Turkey is one of the largest producers of apricots, or kayısı. Because apricots are grown in abundance during the summer months, some of the yearly harvest is dried in the sun to be enjoyed all year round. Malatya, a city in southeast Turkey, is particularly famous for the quality of its dried apricots which are exported all over the world.

When I was a child, we lived in Elazığ, a town next to Malatya and my father would bring home cases of juicy apricots. We would eagerly wait for my father's return from Malatya and the apricots would soon disappear. Apricots are a healthy and nutritious snack, packed with fibre and antioxidants. This dessert is ideal for entertaining, sharing with or just indulging yourself.

Method

Preheat oven to 180°C/350°F/Gas Mark 4

Combine the crushed walnuts and brown sugar in a small bowl as the filling.

Split open the apricots, with a small knife, making sure one end is still intact.

Stuff each apricot with a teaspoonful of crushed walnut and brown sugar mixture and slightly close it up.

Grease a baking tray with a little olive oil or butter and place the stuffed dried apricots on it.

Pour the water over the tray.

Place a tiny little dab of butter on the top of the each stuffed apricot.

Sprinkle brown sugar over the apricots and bake in the oven for 20-25 minutes, until golden brown at top.

Once baked, arrange them in a serving dish and sprinkle over some crushed pistachio nuts.

Afiyet Olsun.

Caramelised carrot paste delight with hazelnuts
Cezerye

Serves 6

Ingredients

3 medium to large carrots (app. 400g/14oz), cleaned and grated

200g/7oz sugar

50g/2oz hazelnuts, chopped into small pieces

240ml/8fl oz water

50g/2oz dessicated coconut flakes to decorate

Small bowl of water to shape cezerye squares or balls

A speciality from the Mersin region of southern Turkey, Cezerye is a confectionery made of carrots, nuts, sugar and coated with dessicated coconut flakes.

High in Vitamin A, this is a healthy dessert that is also thought to be an aphrodisiac. I spent my childhood holidays in Antakya, sampling the very best Cezerye from the nearby Mersin region; it was one of our favourites whenever my cousins and I wanted a treat. They are traditionally made with hazelnuts and easy to make at home. Cezerye keeps well in an airtight container for 3-4 days.

Method

Place the grated carrots, 120ml/4fl oz water and sugar in a wide, heavy pan. Cook over medium heat, uncovered, stirring often. Cook this way for about 30 minutes or until all the liquid has evaporated.

Stir in the rest of the water and cook again on a medium heat, stirring continuously (carrots also release their own juice, therefore I prefer to add the liquid a step at a time so that the carrots won't become mushy).

Cook the carrots until all the juice has evaporated and they are softened, this should take another 30 minutes or so. Using your stirring spoon, mash the cooked carrots to turn into a thick, chunky paste. At this point, they should also thicken, start to caramelise and get sticky (you can take a little bit between your fingers to test whether it sticks or not). Turn the heat off.

Stir in the chopped hazelnuts to the carrot paste and mix well. Again using your stirring spoon, blend them all well and turn into a thick paste.

Cover a small rectangular dish or tray with baking/parchment paper. Spread the carrot paste evenly and tightly, making sure they stay intact, with a height of ½in/1.27cm. Cover with cling film/plastic wrap and rest the mixture to settle for 2 hours in the fridge.

After 2 hours, start shaping the carrot paste. Have a bowl of water near you. Wet your hands, take a dessert spoonful and shape into small spheres. If you don't want to use your hands, wet your knife and cut it into small squares.

Spread the dessicated coconut flakes on a dry surface and roll the carrot balls and squares with the flakes to coat all over.

Cezerye is ready to serve.

Afiyet Olsun.

Candied pumpkin dessert with walnuts
Cevizli Kabak Tatlısı

Serves 6-8

Ingredients

1kg/2¼ lb pumpkin flesh, peeled, deseeded and cut into chunky cubes or rectangular blocks (about 3in/8cm long)

250g/9oz sugar

225g/8oz crushed walnuts to serve

Turkish clotted cream, kaymak or clotted cream to serve (optional)

I enjoy the natural sweetness of pumpkin and this candied pumpkin is a popular dessert in southern Turkey. Baked in its own juice with sugar, this light but full-flavoured pumpkin dessert is best served with crushed walnuts or kaymak (the Turkish thick cream, made from water buffalo milk, available in Middle Eastern stores). If you can't get kaymak, regular clotted cream would work well too.

If you'd like to spice up this dessert, add a few cloves of cinnamon sticks to the juice before baking.

Method

Preheat oven to 180°C/350°F/Gas Mark 4

Line the bottom of a large baking dish with the prepared pumpkin pieces and sprinkle sugar over them evenly. Then layer the rest of the pumpkin chunks and pour the remaining sugar evenly over them. Cover the dish and let it rest overnight.

The next day, you will notice that the pumpkin has released all its juices and that the pieces are nearly covered with all that wonderful juice. This liquid is all you need to bake the pumpkin. There is no need to add any extra water.

Bake the pumpkin in the preheated oven, uncovered. Every 20 minutes, spoon the syrup in the baking dish over the pumpkin pieces so that they all absorb the syrup and start glistening. After 45 minutes of baking, check the sweetness of the pumpkin; if you like it sweeter, you can sprinkle a few more tablespoonfuls of sugar. Also, after 45 minutes of baking, turn the pumpkin pieces around so that all pieces keep moist with the juice. Bake for about 1 hour to 1¼ hours in total, until all the syrup is absorbed and the pumpkin pieces are cooked and candied.

Let the pumpkin dessert cool down. Just before you serve it up, decorate the candied pumpkin pieces with crushed walnuts. You can also serve this delicious dessert with Turkish thick clotted cream, kaymak or regular clotted cream at the side.

Afiyet Olsun.

Antakya's kömbe cookies

Serves 8

Ingredients

500g/1lb 2oz all-purpose/plain flour

200g/7oz unsalted butter, melted

110g/4oz granulated white sugar

2 egg whites, beaten

10ml/2 teaspoons vanilla extract

15ml/1 tablespoon ground cinnamon or kömbe baharat

120ml/4fl oz warm whole milk

For the filling:

85g/3oz crushed walnuts

30ml/2 tablespoons sugar

10ml/2 teaspoons ground cinnamon

45ml/3 tablespoons sesame seeds to decorate

I am passionate about Antakya's kömbe cookies, shaped in intricately carved, wooden kömbe moulds. The Middle Eastern version of kömbe is called mamul or ma'amoul, and is generally baked with dates. There are other ingredient variations in southeast Turkey using crushed nuts or simply baked plain. Regardless of their variations, kömbe cookies and ma'amoul have a special place in Middle Eastern cuisines from weddings to the religious celebrations of Ramadan, Easter, and Hanukkah. Kömbe cookies aren't overly sweet and I think you will enjoy their crunchy bite. My family makes their own kömbe filling with crushed walnuts, sugar and cinnamon. There is a special blend of kömbe baharat in Antakya made with ground cinnamon, all spice, mastic gum, mahlepi, ginger and clove (If you'd like to make your own kömbe baharat, the ratio of cinnamon with the other spices is roughly 3:1).

Method

Preheat oven to 180°C/350°F/Gas Mark 4

Stir in the walnuts, sugar and the ground cinnamon to a small bowl and combine well; the filling is ready.

Combine the flour and the melted butter in a large bowl and mix well. Dissolve the sugar in the warm milk and add to the flour mixture.

Pour in the vanilla extract, egg whites and the cinnamon or kömbe baharat, combine well.

Knead the mixture well for 2-3 minutes, until the dough is soft and smooth.

Take a small walnut size of the dough and press the dough gently into the mould to take its shape. Stuff this dough with about 1 teaspoon of the filling mixture.

Take another small piece of dough, about half of the size of the first one. Flatten and press this dough gently over the filling, to form a cap and close the dough. Press gently and seal the ends of the dough.

Remove the kömbe cookie from the wooden mould by tapping the end of the mould with your fingers firmly and make sure to catch the falling cookie, shaped with the mould's intricate design. Place the cookie on a baking tray and repeat this with the rest of the dough.

Sprinkle sesame seeds over the cookies and press gently. Bake the cookies for about 20 or 25 minutes, until they get a nice light brown colour. They are traditionally lighter in colour.

Once cool, serve the kömbe cookies with tea, çay or Turkish coffee. Kömbe cookies can be stored in an airtight container for at least 3-4 days.

Afiyet Olsun.

Semolina halva with pine nuts
İrmik Helvası

Serves 6-8

Ingredients

110g/4oz unsalted butter

60ml/4 tablespoons light olive oil

450g/1lb coarse semolina – irmik

45ml/3 tablespoons pine nuts

900ml/1½ pints milk – whole milk preferred

335g/12oz sugar

10ml/2 teaspoons ground cinnamon to decorate

15ml/1 tablespoon sautéed pine nuts to decorate

Semolina halva is a traditional dessert made on religious occasions and holy nights in Islam, when it is customary to share the halva with family and friends. İrmik Helvası also signifies good fortune and is made to celebrate events like moving house. In addition, it is traditional for a bereaved family to offer semolina halva to friends when a family member passes away.

Although İrmik Helvası, Semolina Halva, is made with a few simple ingredients, it requires quite a lot of skill to get the consistency right and as such, is often regarded as a culinary masterpiece. The silky blend of buttery semolina with crunchy pine nuts offers a delightful blend of texture and taste, finished off with a dusting of cinnamon.

There are many versions of semolina halva. We Turks prefer a coarse ground semolina, instead of the fine semolina in this halva. You can find coarse semolina in Turkish and Middle Eastern supermarkets, fine semolina is widely available in supermarkets.

Method

Melt the butter and olive oil in a heavy pan, stir in the pine nuts and semolina and cook over a medium heat, stirring all the time, until lightly browned.

At the same time, warm the milk in a separate pan and stir in the sugar. Combine well and let the sugar dissolve. Turn the heat off once the milk is hot (but not boiling) and the sugar is dissolved.

Pour the milk and sugar mixture into semolina and pine nuts mixture and lower the heat. Mix well and cook over a low heat until the milk has been absorbed, stirring continuously for about 10-15 minutes. Turn the heat off. Place a paper towel over the pan and cover with the lid, let the halva rest for about 15 minutes – the paper towel will absorb all the excess moisture.

Sauté 1 tablespoon of pine nuts in a drizzle of olive oil for a few minutes. Spoon the semolina halva into individual bowls, and serve with a dusting of cinnamon and a few sautéed pine nuts over them.

Afiyet Olsun.

Homemade Turkish delight
Lokum

Makes about 64 small squares

Ingredients

25g/1oz icing sugar

100g/3½ oz corn flour

700g/1½ lb caster sugar

Juice of 1 lemon

45ml/3 tablespoons powdered (vegetarian) gelatine

30ml/2 tablespoons rose water

Gold edible glitter – optional

Have you ever tried genuine Turkish delight, Lokum? These delicately flavoured sweets has been a hallmark of Turkey since Ottoman times. Prepared plain (sade), or delicately flavoured with rose water, or using dried fruits, nuts and dessicated coconut are common ingredients often used in Turkish delight. Sakız (mastic gum) is used to create a chewier version of Turkish delight and also with the rolled up version of lokum.

We make Turkish delight at my cookery classes and it is always a big hit. You need to allow for the fragrant jelly to set at least overnight (and more if you can).

This recipe makes plain (sade) Turkish delight with a softer texture than that sold in the shops. Don't be scared to experiment adding chopped hazelnuts, pistachios or walnuts to the jelly before it sets.

Method

Line an 8in/20.5cm square baking tin with cling film/plastic wrap. Sift icing sugar and 25g/1oz of the cornflour into a small bowl. Sprinkle a little over the base and sides of the tin. Set bowl aside.

Put the caster sugar, lemon juice and 400ml/14fl oz of water into large pan. Heat gently until dissolved – do not boil. In a small bowl, mix the remaining corn flour with 100ml/3½fl oz of cold water, and then stir into sugar syrup. Sprinkle the gelatine over the liquid and stir with a balloon whisk to break up any lumps. Bring to the boil, then simmer over a medium heat for 20 minutes, whisking often. The mixture should thicken and turn pale yellow.

Remove from the heat and set aside for 5 minutes. Stir in the rose water and pour into the tin. Leave it to set in a cool place overnight.

Dust a board with some reserved cornflour mixture, and then invert the Turkish delight on to it. Remove tin; peel off the cling film/plastic wrap. Cut into cubes, and then roll each gently into the cornflour mixture to coat.

Sprinkle over a little glitter, if using. Store in an airtight container with remaining cornflour mixture at cool room temperature for up to 1 month. To pack as gifts, sprinkle a little corn flour mixture into a bag to stop the sweets sticking.

Afiyet Olsun.

Turkish coffee
Türk kahvesi

You'll hear me say over and over that Turkish coffee is a very special drink. It really is more than a drink with its proud history, traditions and rituals. We have a saying "Bir fincan kahvenin kırk yıl hatırı vardır", which means "The memory of a good cup of Turkish coffee lasts 40 years". Turkish coffee is a drink that is best drunk with friends or friends to be. In Turkey you are offered this traditional, aromatic beverage wherever you go. So, this could be when visiting friends and family, in the shops, while waiting in the bank and even in the hairdressers. We take time to pause and enjoy Turkish coffee with every precious sip. We look back to the things of the past, live in the moment and look forward with anticipation to the future. A glass of water and Turkish delights, Lokum by the side, complete the ritual.

Turkish coffee is made from 100 per cent Arabica beans that have to be toasted to the roasting point and ground to a very fine powder. When properly made, a delicious foam forms at the top, which is essential to any Turkish coffee. My mother loves her daily Turkish coffee but needs to limit herself to one a day. If she is ordering in a café, she charmingly asks the waiter for a "güzel köpüklü Türk kahvesi lütfen", which means "Turkish coffee with a nice foam at the top please." That is her precious treat for the day.

The traditional first step in a Turkish marriage proposal, unsurprisingly, also starts with Turkish coffee. The bride-to-be makes the Turkish coffee for her prospective groom when he visits her father seeking permission for his daughter's hand in marriage. Custom stipulates the coffee served must have a nice frothy cream on top. I took this test when my husband asked my father's permission. Despite all the Turkish coffees I've made in my life, I must admit that one was a little bit nerve racking. Happily I passed the test and with flying colours.

Method

To make Turkish coffee, you need the right equipment: a special long handled pot called cezve and small coffee cups, similar to espresso size cups called fincan. The size of the pot is significant. It must hold almost double the amount of the water used to have adequate "room" on the top for the foam to rise.

Put one coffee cup of water for each person, 1 heaped teaspoon of Turkish coffee and 1 rounded teaspoon or less of sugar in to your cezve, long handled pot. Traditionally, the amount of sugar should be known beforehand, e.g. az şekerli (with a little sugar), orta şekerli (medium), or şekersiz or sade (with no sugar) Skip the sugar if preferred. Stir well, put over a low heat and bring slowly to the boil.

As it gently starts to boil, the froth forms on top and rises. Just before it overflows, remove and divide the froth into the cups. Then bring to the boil again and divide the rest out to the cups. Sit back and savour the flavour and the glorious aroma. Your Turkish coffee, Türk kahvesi, is ready.

Turkish delight, lokum traditionally accompanies the Turkish coffee and it is a perfect fit.

Afiyet Olsun.

Chapter Twelve

Suggested Menus

Suggested Menus

Traditional Turkish Dinner Menu

Spicy lentil and bulgur soup
Ezo Gelin Çorbası

Tray bake spinach and cheese filo pastry
Ispanaklı, Peynirli Börek

Warm hummus with red pepper flakes infused olive oil
Humus

Shepherd's salad with sumac
Sumaklı Çoban Salata

Baked Turkish meatballs with vegetables
Fırında Sebzeli Köfte

Baklava with pistachios & walnuts
Fıstıklı ve Cevizli Baklava

Turkish coffee or Turkish tea
Türk kahvesi or çay

Vegetarian Feast Menu

Oval flat breads with cheese, peppers, onions and spinach
Peynirli, Sebzeli Pide

Green beans cooked in olive oil with vegetables
Zeytinyağlı Taze Fasülye

Bulgur pilaf with courgette/zucchini, onions and tomatoes
Kabaklı Aş

Diced cucumbers, yoghurt and dried mint dip
Cacık dip

Zesty semolina sponge cake in syrup
Revani

Turkish coffee or Turkish tea
Türk kahvesi or çay

Gluten-free Menu

Baked sea bass with vegetables in olive oil
Fırında Sebzeli Levrek

Aubergines/eggplants, lentils and peppers cooked in olive oil
Mercimekli Mualla

Gavurdağı salad with pomegranate molasses

Dried baked apricots with walnuts
Cevizli Kuru Kayısı Tatlısı

Turkish coffee or Turkish tea
Türk kahvesi or çay

Southern Turkish themed menu for entertaining

Walnut and red pepper paste dip
Muhammara – Cevizli Biber

Tahini bread with sesame and nigella seeds
Tahinli Ekmek

Spicy bulgur wheat salad with pomegranate molasses
Kısır

Leafy greens with onions, peppers and pine nuts
Antakya's Zılk Inspiration

Upside down rice with layers of chicken, aubergine/eggplant and potatoes
Mevlübi

Syrup soaked, cheese filled pastry strands
Künefe

Turkish coffee or Turkish tea
Türk kahvesi or çay

Suggested Menus

Meze Menu

Olive salad with pomegranate molasses and za'atar
Zeytin Üfeleme

Baked spinach and cheese filo triangles
Muska Böreği

Radish salad with tahini sauce
Tahinli Turp Salatası

Courgette/zucchini fritters with feta and dill
Kabak Mücveri

Baked prawns with onions, peppers, mushroom and tomatoes
Karides Güveç

Baked mini Turkish style meatballs in tomato and red pepper sauce
Mini Sebzeli Köfte

Caramelised carrot paste delight with hazelnuts
Cezerye

Turkish coffee or Turkish tea
Türk kahvesi or çay

Kebab Menu

Sautéed carrots and parsley with garlic yoghurt
Sarımsak Yoğurtlu Havuç

Smoked aubergine/eggplant salad with tomatoes, onions, peppers
Patlıcanlı Ekşileme

Minced/ground lamb kebabs with pistachios and roasted vegetables
Fıstıklı Kebap

Baked cauliflower with red onions, feta and dill
Fırında Karnabahar Mücveri

Candied pumpkin dessert with walnuts
Cevizli Kabak Tatlısı

Turkish coffee or Turkish tea
Türk kahvesi or çay

Ozerlat UK – Turkish Delights

Acknowledgements

This special book has been my vision and my dream. Since I started my Turkish cookery blog, Özlem's Turkish Table, 9 years ago, I have had a burning desire to publish my recipes showcasing my southern Turkish roots and spread the word on delicious Turkish cuisine. Making a book is a labour of love and some very special thanks are in order for many dear people in my life, who helped my wish come true.

My dear mum and dad, Gülçin and Orhan; I can't thank you enough for your continuous love, support and inspiration, this book is your legacy and I am so happy to pass it on to the next generations. My dearest husband Angus and our lovely children Mark Can and Emma Gülçin; I am ever grateful for all your support, love and patience. It means the world to me and big thanks from the heart - I couldn't do this without you all.

My dear sister Öznur, gorgeous sister-in-law Judith and all my extended family for their invaluable support and inspiration. My dear cousin Suphi Ural for black and white family photos, my very talented cousins Nihal Sarıoğlu and Ahmet Sabuncu for all their support and creative feedback.

My very special thanks goes to my publisher GB Publishing, George Boughton and Brenda Marsh for believing in me and all their very precious support. You lit the fire and I am ever grateful. Dear Sian Irvine; huge thanks for your amazing food photography, your passion and support for this very special book, you are one amazing photographer. Our super-efficient Production Manager; Katy Banyard, our very talented Art Director and Designer; Holly Tillier, sincere thanks for project managing and making the book come alive so beautifully. Our talented Editor; Will Campbell and Associate Editor; my dear friend Gillian Burns for their meticulous editing, suggestions and continuous love and care to shape the book, my heartfelt thanks.

A very sincere, çok teşekkürler to dear Ghillie Başan for your Foreword; your amazing books on Turkish cookery continue to be an inspiration for me and you have always been a rôle- model. I am ever grateful to all your support and kindness. Angie Mitchell, Jale Balcı, Nursen Doğan and Somer Sivrioğlu; sincere thanks to you all too as I love and often turn to your wonderful Turkish cookery books.

ZEN Ceramics team and my dear cousin Nihal Sarıoğlu for the beautiful ZEN Ceramics plates from Turkey, Divertimenti in London, The Kitchen Shop in Weybridge, Surrey and dear İnci Malik and Aromas Artisan Kitchen in Weybridge, lovely Nest Home and Café in Ripley, Surrey for all your gorgeous plates and bowls that we used in the book.

My very special thanks goes to Claudia Turgut, the original owner of the wonderful blog, Seasonal Cook in Turkey.

Claudia very kindly let us use a large variety of her location photography, including some wonderful double page spreads, which I am deeply grateful. She meticulously searched photos from her library for the different sections of the book; from beautiful food and market spreads to gorgeous shots of Istanbul and Bosphorus, her shots are much treasured. Another passionate photographer, Katherine Baker, also kindly shared her beautiful shots throughout the book, including our lovely cookery class photos in Zekeriyaköy, Istanbul. They are all very special contributions and my very sincere thanks goes to her. Many thanks also to Ismail Daşgeldi, Joy Ludwig-Mcnutt from My Traveling Joys, Nancy Laing, Julia Power from Turkey's For Life, Lyn Ward from Fethiye Times for letting us use their lovely images. My special thanks also to Nadia Swindell Photography for my professional photo that I use all the time.

Ozerlat UK for the Turkish coffee and Turkish delight images and Secret Gardens Organic Pomegranate Essence for their delicious pomegranate essence from Antakya.

Dear friends Mark and Jolee – ex Senior Dogs - Sarah Hills, Suhair Kilani from Pantera – Jordan, Turkish Embassy in Amman – Jordan, Perinaz Avari from the delicious Peri's Spice Ladle, Ece Erimez, Özlem Kalaycıoğlu, Handan Sadıkoğlu, Lela Jane – Lillis, Veronica Gonzales, Ilgen Paydas from Cotton & Olive, Mary Suphi, Julia Britten, Julia Richards, Nejla Engin, Pamela Wood, Hande Castiglione, Nuray Aykın, Tricia Woolfrey, Tom Evans, Natalie Lefebvre, Tone Tellefsen Hughes, Mariette Jansen, Gülsüm Genç Koç, Mete Ucer, Jill Bennett, Sarah Hodge, Sema Sagat, Ceylan Kıral Ayık, Petek Çırpılı, Mark Ulyseas – Live Encounters magazine, Nichola Craven and Linnea Woolfson for all your inspiration, encouragement, lending plates and support.

Also, my dear friends Leonie Wright, Claire Fitzsimons, Ellie Harrison, Ann Holliday, Mina Hoad and Heleen Koolhof for helping out during our photo shoots. A very special thanks to dear Susie Bossard, for all her help leading to the photo shoots and beyond. I couldn't have done this without all of you.

Last but not least, my dear blogger friends from Turkey; we have been on this blogging journey together - Annie Onursan from Back to Bodrum, Alan Fenn from Archers of Okcular, Natalie Sayın from Turkish Travel Blog and Julia & Barry from Turkey's For Life, Roving Jay and all blogger friends for your encouragement, support and belief in me.

Çok teşekkürler to you all.

Index